SEXUAL DISCRIMINATION AND HARASSMENT

SEXUAL DISCRIMINATION AND HARASSMENT

RACHEL C. FELDMAN
EDITOR

Nova Science Publishers, Inc.
New York

NOTICE TO THE READER
The Publisher has taken reasonable care in the preparation of this book, but makes no expressed or implied warranty of any kind and assumes no responsibility for any errors or omissions. No liability is assumed for incidental or consequential damages in connection with or arising out of information contained in this book. The Publisher shall not be liable for any special, consequential, or exemplary damages resulting, in whole or in part, from the readers' use of, or reliance upon, this material.

Independent verification should be sought for any data, advice or recommendations contained in this book. In addition, no responsibility is assumed by the publisher for any injury and/or damage to persons or property arising from any methods, products, instructions, ideas or otherwise contained in this publication.

This publication is designed to provide accurate and authoritative information with regard to the subject matter covered herein. It is sold with the clear understanding that the Publisher is not engaged in rendering legal or any other professional services. If legal or any other expert assistance is required, the services of a competent person should be sought. FROM A DECLARATION OF PARTICIPANTS JOINTLY ADOPTED BY A COMMITTEE OF THE AMERICAN BAR ASSOCIATION AND A COMMITTEE OF PUBLISHERS.

LIBRARY OF CONGRESS CATALOGING-IN-PUBLICATION DATA
Sexual discrimination and harrassment / Rachel C. Feldman (editor).
   p. cm.
 Includes bibliographical references.
 ISBN 978-1-60456-380-1 (hardcover)
 1. Sex discrimination--Law and legislation--United States. 2. Sexual harassment--Law and legislation--United States. I. Feldman, Rachel C.
 KF4758.S49   2008
 342.7308'78--dc22   2007052100

Published by Nova Science Publishers, Inc. ✦ New York

CONTENTS

PREFACE

The Sex Discrimination Act 1984 prohibits discrimination on the basis of sex, marital status, pregnancy or potential pregnancy in a range of areas of public life. These areas include work, accommodation, education, the provision of goods, facilities and services, the activities of clubs and the administration of Commonwealth laws and programs.

Among other things, the Sex Discrimination Act seeks to eliminate discrimination involving dismissal of employees with family responsibilities and to eliminate sexual harassment in areas of public activity.

Recognition and acceptance within the community of the principle of the equality of men and women is also a goal of the Sex Discrimination Act.

Chapter 1 - Gender-based discrimination, sexual harassment, and violence against women in the workplace, schools, and society at large are continuing topics of legislative and judicial concern. Legal doctrines condemning the extortion of sexual favors as a condition of employment or job advancement and other sexually offensive workplace behaviors resulting in a "hostile environment" have evolved from judicial decisions under Title VII of the 1964 Civil Rights Act and other federal equal employment opportunity laws. The earlier judicial focus on economic detriment or *quid pro quo* harassment — i.e., making submission to sexual demands a condition of job benefits — has largely given way to Title VII claims alleging harassment that creates an "intimidating, hostile, or offensive environment." Under Title IX of the Education Amendments of 1972, victims of sexual harassment that occurs in a public school setting may make similar *quid pro quo* or hostile environment claims.

Chapter 2 - In its sex discrimination decisions, the United States Supreme Court not only has defined the applicability of the equal protection guarantees of the Constitution and the nondiscriminatory policies of federal statutes, but also has rejected the use of gender stereotypes and has continued to recognize the discriminatory effect of gender hostility in the workplace and in schools. This report focuses on recent sex discrimination challenges based on: the equal protection guarantees of the Fourteenth and Fifth Amendments; the prohibition against employment discrimination contained in Title VII of the Civil Rights Act of 1964; and the prohibition against sex discrimination in education contained in Title IX of the Education Amendments of 1972. Although this report focuses on recent legal developments in each of these areas, this report also provides historical context by discussing selected landmark sex discrimination cases.

Despite the fact that the Court's analysis of sex discrimination challenges under the Constitution differs from its analysis of sex discrimination under the two federal statutes discussed in this report, it is apparent that the Court is willing to refine its standards of review under both schemes to accommodate the novel claims presented by these cases. The Court's decisions in cases involving Title VII and Title IX are particularly noteworthy because they illustrate the Court's recognition of sexual harassment in both the workplace and the classroom.

Chapter 3 - The U.N. Convention on the Elimination of All Forms of Discrimination Against Women calls for Parties to eliminate discrimination against women in all areas of life, including healthcare, education, employment, domestic relations, law, commercial transactions, and political participation. As of November 2, 2006, the Convention was ratified or acceded to by 185 countries.

President Jimmy Carter submitted the Convention to the Senate in 1980. The Senate Foreign Relations Committee held hearings on the Convention in 1988, 1990, 1994, and 2002, but the treaty was never considered for ratification by the full Senate. The George W. Bush Administration began conducting a full legal and policy review of the Convention in 2002. On February 7, 2007, the Administration transmitted a letter to the Senate Foreign Relations Committee stating that it does not support Senate action on the treaty at this time.

U.S. ratification of CEDAW is a contentious policy issue that has generated considerable debate in Congress and among the general public. Supporters of U.S. ratification contend that the Convention is a valuable mechanism for fighting women's discrimination worldwide. They argue that U.S. ratification of the treaty will give the Convention additional legitimacy, and that it will further empower women who fight discrimination in other countries. Opponents of ratification contend that the Convention is not the best or most efficient way to eliminate discrimination against women. They believe ratification will undermine U.S. sovereignty and impact U.S. social policy related to family planning and abortion.

This report provides background on CEDAW developments, including U.S. policy and congressional actions, and considers arguments for and against ratification.

Chapter 4 - H.R. 3685, passed by the House on November 7, 2007, would prohibit certain adverse employment actions taken against an individual because of that individual's actual or perceived sexual orientation. Referred to as the Employment NonDiscrimination Act of 2007 (ENDA), the bill also explicitly prohibits employment discrimination against an individual based upon the sexual orientation of persons associated with that individual, but does not permit disparate impact claims of sexual orientation discrimination. A substantial minority of states have enacted their own prohibitions against sexual orientation employment discrimination. Some instances of sexual orientation employment discrimination may also be prohibited by existing protections under Title VII of the Civil Rights Act of 1964, despite the fact that Title VII's definition of sex does not encompass sexual orientation. H.R. 3685 would also appear to exempt religious organizations as defined under Title VII.

In: Sexual Discrimination and Harassment   ISBN: 978-1-60456-380-1
Editor: Rachel C. Feldman, pp. 1-36   © 2008 Nova Science Publishers, Inc.

Chapter 1

SEXUAL HARASSMENT: DEVELOPMENTS IN FEDERAL LAW[1]*

Jody Feder

ABSTRACT

Gender-based discrimination, sexual harassment, and violence against women in the workplace, schools, and society at large are continuing topics of legislative and judicial concern. Legal doctrines condemning the extortion of sexual favors as a condition of employment or job advancement and other sexually offensive workplace behaviors resulting in a "hostile environment" have evolved from judicial decisions under Title VII of the 1964 Civil Rights Act and other federal equal employment opportunity laws. The earlier judicial focus on economic detriment or *quid pro quo* harassment — i.e., making submission to sexual demands a condition of job benefits — has largely given way to Title VII claims alleging harassment that creates an "intimidating, hostile, or offensive environment." Under Title IX of the Education Amendments of 1972, victims of sexual harassment that occurs in a public school setting may make similar *quid pro quo* or hostile environment claims.

---

* Excerpted from CRS Report RL33736, dated November 27, 2006.

INTRODUCTION

Gender-based discrimination, sexual harassment, and violence against women in the workplace, schools, and society at large are continuing topics of legislative and judicial concern. Legal doctrines condemning the extortion of sexual favors as a condition of employment or job advancement and other sexually offensive workplace behaviors resulting in a "hostile environment" have evolved from judicial decisions under Title VII of the 1964 Civil Rights Act and other federal equal employment opportunity laws.[2] The earlier judicial focus on economic detriment or *quid pro quo* harassment — i.e., making submission to sexual demands a condition of job benefits — has largely given way to Title VII claims alleging harassment that creates an "intimidating, hostile, or offensive environment." Under Title IX of the Education Amendments of 1972,[3] victims of sexual harassment that occurs in a public school setting may make similar *quid pro quo* or hostile environment claims.

In recent years, the U.S. Supreme Court has addressed a range of sexual harassment issues from the legality of same-sex harassment to the vicarious liability of employers and local school districts for monetary damages as the result of harassment by supervisors and teachers. These and other significant Supreme Court cases regarding sexual harassment and violence against women are discussed below.

FEDERAL EQUAL EMPLOYMENT OPPORTUNITY LAW

Title VII of the 1964 Civil Rights Act does not mention sexual harassment but makes it unlawful for employers with 15 or more employees to discriminate against any applicant or employee "because of ... sex."[4] Federal law on the subject is, therefore, largely a judicial creation, having evolved over four decades from federal court decisions and guidelines of the Equal Employment Opportunity Commission (EEOC) interpreting Title VII's sex discrimination prohibition.[5] Sexual harassment in federally assisted education programs is also prohibited by Title IX of the 1972 Education Amendments.[6] While Title VII and Title IX are the primary sources of federal sexual harassment law, relief from such conduct has also been sought, albeit less frequently, pursuant to § 1983 of Title 42, the Federal Employees Liability Act, and the Equal Protection and Due Process Clauses of the U.S. Constitution.[7]

Two forms of sexual harassment have been recognized by the courts and EEOC administrative guidelines. The first, or *"quid pro quo"* harassment, occurs when submission to "unwelcome" sexual advances, propositions, or other conduct of a sexual nature is made an express or implied condition of employment, or where it is used as the basis of employment decisions affecting job status or tangible employment benefits. As its name suggests, this form of harassment involves actual or potential economic loss — such as termination, transfer, or adverse performance ratings — as a consequence of the employee's refusal to exchange sexual favors demanded by a supervisor or employer for employment benefits. The second form of actionable harassment consists of unwelcome sexual conduct that is of such severity as to alter a condition of employment by creating an "intimidating, hostile, or offensive working environment." The essence of a "hostile environment" claim is a "pattern or practice" of offensive behavior by the employer, a supervisor, coworkers, or non-employees so "severe or pervasive" as to interfere with the employee's job performance or create an abusive work environment.

In 1980, the federal agency responsible for enforcing Title VII issued guidelines prohibiting both *quid pro quo* and hostile environment sexual harassment.[8] The EEOC guidelines focus on sexuality rather than gender — in terms of job detriments resulting from "[u]nwelcome sexual advances, requests for sexual favors, and other verbal or physical behavior of a sexual nature"   and require that a "totality of the circumstances" be considered to determine whether particular conduct constitutes sexual harassment.[9] In addition, the EEOC anticipated judicial developments in hostile environment law when it eliminated tangible economic loss as a factor and provided that unwelcome sexual conduct violates Title VII whenever it "has the purpose or effect of unreasonably interfering with an individual's work performance or creating an intimidating, hostile, or offensive working environment." According to the EEOC guidelines, an employer is liable for both forms of sexual harassment when perpetrated by supervisors. The employer, however, is liable for harassment perpetrated by co-worker or nonemployees only if the employer knew or should have known of the harassment and failed to "take immediate and appropriate corrective action." They also recommend that employers take preventive measures to eliminate sexual harassment and state that employers may be liable to those denied employment opportunities or benefits given to another employee because of submission to sexual advances.[10]

In 1990, the EEOC issued policy guidance to elaborate on certain legal principles set forth in its interpretative guidelines from a decade before.[11] First, the later document reasserted the basic distinction between "quid pro quo" and "hostile environment" and states that an employer "will always be held responsible for acts of '*quid pro quo*' harassment" by a supervisor while hostile environment cases require "careful examination" of whether the harassing supervisor was acting in an `agency capacity.'"[12] On the "welcomeness" issue, the policy guide states that "a contemporaneous complaint or protest" by the victim is an "important" but "not a necessary element of the claim." Instead, the Commission will look to all "objective evidence, rather than subjective, uncommunicated feelings" to "determine whether the victim's conduct is consistent, or inconsistent, with her assertion that the sexual conduct is unwelcome."[13] In determining whether a work environment is hostile, several factors are emphasized:

(1) whether the conduct was verbal or physical or both; (2) how frequently it was repeated; (3) whether the conduct was hostile or patently offensive; (4) whether the alleged harasser was a co-worker or supervisor; (5) whether others joined in perpetrating the harassment; and (6) whether the harassment was directed at more than one individual.

However, because the alleged misconduct must "substantially interfere" with the victim's job performance, "sexual flirtation or innuendo, even vulgar language that is trivial or merely annoying, would probably not establish a hostile environment." In addition, "the harasser's conduct should be evaluated from the objective standard of a 'reasonable person.'"[14]

In 1999, the EEOC rescinded the employer liability rules of these earlier documents, in line with the *Faragher* and *Ellerth* decisions discussed below. The latest guidelines apply the same liability principles to all forms or illegal harassment — whether based on race, color, sex, religion, national origin, age, or disability —prohibited by federal anti-discrimination statutes.[15] In terms of substantive scope, the guidance emphasizes that harassment targeted against an individual because of sex need not involve sexual comments or conduct to be actionable. For example, the EEOC states that frequent, derogatory remarks about women may constitute unlawful harassment even if they are nonsexual in nature so long as they are sufficiently pervasive and are directed only at female (or male) employees because of their sex. Both the "supervisor" and "tangible employment action" necessary for imputing vicarious employer liability are broadly defined. Thus, the former includes any individual who has, or is regarded to have, the authority to affect an employee's work activities or status, whether directly or by recommendation to a final decision-maker. The latter refers to any job detriment or benefit that results in significant change in employment status (e.g., a pay raise in exchange for sexual favors), but an unfulfilled threat by a supervisor is insufficient to be a "tangible employment action."

In addition, the employer has a duty of "reasonable care" to prevent and remedy harassment and, unless a very small employer, must establish, disseminate, and enforce a formal anti-harassment policy and complaint procedure, among other steps. Even an employer that promptly responds to a complaint has not taken reasonable care if it ignored prior complaints by other employees, or if it fails to screen supervisory applicants for any prior record of engaging in harassment. A harassment victim, on the other hand, must take advantage of any policy and procedures provided by the employer, and may be denied full monetary relief if she unreasonably delays in complaining. An employee may reasonably be excused from complaining, or for delay in doing so, only where there appears to be a risk of retaliation or other built-in obstacles making the complaint mechanism ineffective.

QUID PRO QUO HARASSMENT

The earliest judicial challenges involving tangible job detriment or *quid pro quo* harassment claims — filed by women who were allegedly fired for resisting sexual advances by their supervisors — were largely unsuccessful. The discriminatory conduct in such cases was deemed to arise from "personal proclivity" of the supervisor rather than "company directed policy which deprived women of employment opportunities." Until the mid-1970's, federal district courts were reluctant either to find a Title VII cause of action or to impose liability on employers who were neither in complicity with, nor had actual knowledge of, *quid pro quo* harassment by their supervisory employees. An historic turning point came when the federal district court in *Williams v. Saxbe* held for the first time that sexual harassment was discriminatory treatment within the meaning of Title VII because "it created an artificial barrier to employment which was placed before one gender and not the other, despite the fact that both genders were similarly situated."[16] Echoing earlier opinions that an employer is not liable for "interpersonal disputes between employees," the court nonetheless refused to dismiss the complaint since "if [the alleged harassment] was a policy or practice of plaintiff's supervisor, then it was the agency's policy or practice, which is prohibited by Title VII."[17]

Appellate tribunals in several federal circuits soon began to affirm that *quid pro quo* harassment violates Title VII where "gender is a substantial factor in the discrimination," reversing contrary lower court holdings. For example, in *Barnes v. Costle*, the D.C. Circuit disagreed with "the notion that employment conditions summoning sexual relations are somehow exempted from the coverage of Title VII."[18] Finding that it was "enough that gender is a factor contributing to the discrimination in a substantial way," the court ruled that differential treatment based upon an employee's rejection of her supervisor's sexual advances violated the statute. Similarly, in *Tomkins v. Public Service Electric and Gas Co.*, the Third Circuit reversed the trial court's denial of Title VII protection to all "sexual harassment and sexually motivated assault," finding that where an employee's "status as a female was a motivating factor in the supervisor's conditioning her continued employment on compliance with his sexual demands," actionable *quid pro quo* harassment had occurred. "[T]o establish a *prima facie* case of *quid pro quo* harassment, a plaintiff must present evidence that she was subject to unwelcome sexual conduct, and that her reaction to that conduct was then used as the basis for decisions affecting the compensation, terms, conditions, or privileges of her employment."[19]

Where the conduct of the alleged harasser is motivated by factors other than the sex of the plaintiff, however, there may be no *quid pro quo* harassment. So-called "paramour" cases are a prime example. In *Piech v. Arthur Anderson and Co.*,[20] the court held that the plaintiff's inability to obtain a promotion, given instead to a female co-worker who was romantically involved with the employer, did not result from sex discrimination since all other employees, male or female, were equally affected. In contrast, the claim that females employed by the defendant had to extend sexual favors to succeed was cognizable as *quid pro quo* harassment. *Ellert v. University of Texas[21]* similarly held that a secretary could not establish a *quid pro quo* harassment claim by alleging that her discharge resulted from her knowledge of the university dean's unwelcome advances towards an associate. Even if the plaintiff's knowledge of the affair was the basis of action taken against her, it was not motivated by her gender and thus was not prohibited by Title VII.

While the loss of a "tangible employment benefit" has most often meant dismissal or demotion, *quid pro quo* claims may also arise from denial of career advantages — job title, duties, or assignments — of less immediate economic impact upon the employee. The Seventh Circuit, for example, has ruled that a tenured professor who was allegedly stripped of her job title and removed from academic committees because she rebuffed the sexual advances of the university provost may have a claim for *quid pro quo* sexual harassment under Title VII.[22] By contrast, the Fourth Circuit vacated a judgment in favor of the plaintiff in *Reingold v. Virginia*,[23] concluding that assigning her extra work, giving her inappropriate work assignments not included in her job description, and denying her the opportunity to attend a professional conference, did not amount to a "significant change in employment status." Generally speaking, the more remote or insubstantial the consequences of refusing a supervisor's unwelcome advances, the less likely that prerequisites for a *quid pro quo* will be found.[24]

The dismissal by Judge Susan Weber Wright of Paula Jones' sexual harassment lawsuit against former-President Clinton squarely addressed the workplace consequences that must flow from the refusal to submit to an unwelcome sexual advance for the court to find actionable harassment.[25] Plaintiff Jones claimed that her career advancement had repeatedly been thwarted by her state employer as retribution for rebuffing the former Arkansas Governor. As evidence of "tangible job detriments," Jones alleged that she had been discouraged by supervisors from seeking job promotions or pay increases; that following return from maternity leave, she was transferred to a new position with fewer responsibilities; that she was effectively denied access to grievance procedures available to other sexual harassment victims; and that by physically isolating her directly outside her supervisor's office with little work to do, she was "subjected to hostile treatment having tangible effects." Judge Wright was unconvinced by the record, however, that any threat perceived by Jones during her alleged hotel meeting with the former Governor was so "clear and unambiguous" as to be a *quid pro quo* conditioning of "concrete job benefits or detriments on compliance with sexual demands." "Refusal" cases like *Jones*, calling for proof of "tangible job detriment" by plaintiffs who resist unwelcome sexual demands,[26] were distinguished from so-called "submission" cases, where "in the nature of things, economic harm will not be available to support the claim of the employee who submits to the supervisor's demands."[27]

It was widely anticipated that some further guidance on the essential character of *quid pro quo* harassment, particularly in relation to Jones' claims against President Clinton, would be forthcoming when the Supreme Court decided *Burlington Industries, Inc. v. Ellerth.[28]* That case involved a former merchandising assistant at Burlington Industries who alleged that she was the subject of repeated boorish and offensive comments and gestures by a division vice-president who implied that her response to his advances would affect her career. Ellerth detailed three incidents in which her supervisor's comments could be construed as threats to deny her tangible job benefits. A short time later, she quit her job without informing anyone in authority about the harassment, even though she was aware of Burlington's anti-harassment policy. Squarely presented by *Ellerth*, therefore, was the question of whether sexual advances by a supervisor accompanied by the threatened but not actualized loss of employment or job benefits may render an employer liable for *quid pro quo* harassment.

In fashioning an employer liability rule in *Ellerth*, the Court considered the judicial distinction between *quid pro quo* and environmental harassment to be less important than whether the claim involved a threat that had been "carried out" in fact.[29] Such actions, according to the Court, include instances where the subordinate employee is subjected to "a significant change in employment status, such as hiring, firing, failing to promote, reassignment with significantly different responsibilities, or a decision causing a significant change in benefits" for failing to permit sexual liberties.[30] Claims based on unfulfilled threats of retaliation were equated by the Court to hostile environment harassment, requiring plaintiff to prove "severe and pervasive" conduct.

Since Ellerth had not demonstrated that she was the victim of retaliation by her supervisor — in fact, she had been promoted during the period in question — there was no tangible detriment for which the employer could be held strictly liable. The case was remanded, however, for application of an alternative standard of vicarious employer liability formulated by the Court for supervisory harassment cases not involving a "tangible employment action." Under that rule, after the plaintiff proves that the supervisory misconduct is both "severe and pervasive," the employer may assert as an "affirmative defense" that its actions to prevent and remedy workplace harassment were "reasonable," while the plaintiff "unreasonably" failed to take advantage of any anti-harassment policies and procedures of the employer. Ellerth's failure to avail herself of the employer's grievance procedure likely defeated any Title VII recovery against Burlington under the second prong of this defense. The judicial task for lower courts after *Ellerth* is to construe this duty of reasonable care governing the employer's affirmative defense to liability. Other than rewarding employers for prophylactic measures aimed at workplace harassment and compelling victim participation in those efforts, *Ellerth* provides little specific guidance.

Hostile Environment Harassment

The earlier judicial focus on economic detriment or *quid pro quo* harassment —making submission to sexual demands a condition to job benefits — largely gave way to Title VII claims for harassment that create an "intimidating, hostile, or offensive environment." The first federal appellate court to jettison the tangible economic loss requirement and recognize a hostile environment claim of sexual harassment was the D.C. Circuit in *Bundy v. Jackson*.[31] Despite the plaintiff's failure to prove *quid pro quo* harassment — she was not fired, demoted, or denied a promotion — the court refused to permit an employer to lawfully harass an employee "by carefully stopping short of firing the employee or taking any other tangible actions against her in response to her resistance."[32] Another decision important to the judicial development of sexually hostile environment law was *Henson v. Dundee*, in which the Eleventh Circuit rejected a claim of *quid pro quo* harassment but found that the employee had a right to a trial on the merits to determine whether the misconduct alleged made her job environment hostile.[33]

In *Meritor Savings Bank v. Vinson*,[34] the Supreme Court ratified the consensus then emerging among the federal circuits by recognizing a Title VII cause of action for sexual harassment. According to the Court, a "hostile environment," predicated on "purely psychological aspects of the workplace environment," could give rise to legal liability, and "tangible loss" of "an economic character" was not an essential element.[35] This holding was qualified by the Court with important reservations drawn from earlier administrative and judicial precedent. First, "not all workplace conduct that can be described as 'harassment' affects a term, condition, or privilege of employment within the meaning of Title VII." For example, the "mere utterance" of an "epithet" engendering "offensive feelings in an employee" would not ordinarily be *per se* actionable, the opinion suggests. Rather, the misconduct "must be sufficiently severe or pervasive to alter the conditions of [the victim's] employment and create an abusive working environment."[36]

Second, while "voluntariness" in the sense of consent is not a defense to a sexual harassment charge,

> [t]he gravamen of any sexual harassment claim is that the alleged sexual advances were 'unwelcome.' ... The correct inquiry is whether respondent by her conduct indicated that the alleged sexual advances were unwelcome, not whether her actual participation in sexual intercourse was voluntary.[37]

Accordingly, "it does not follow that a complainant's sexually provocative speech or dress is irrelevant as a matter of law in determining whether he or she found particular sexual advances unwelcome. To the contrary, such evidence is obviously relevant."[38]

On the question of employer liability, the *Meritor Savings* majority held that the court below had "erred in concluding that employers are always automatically liable for sexual harassment by their supervisors."[39] The usual rule in Title VII cases is strict liability, and four Justices, concurring in the judgment, argued that the same rule should apply in the sexual harassment context as well. The majority disagreed, impliedly suggesting that in hostile environment cases no employer, at least none with a formal policy against harassment, should be made liable in the absence of actual or constructive knowledge.

The Supreme Court's failure to clearly define what constitutes a hostile environment in *Meritor Savings* led to frequent conflict in the lower courts, particularly as to the necessity of proving that serious psychological injury resulted from the harassing conduct.[40] The Court's decision in *Harris v. Forklift Systems, Inc.* revisited and offered some clarification of *Meritor Savings* in this regard.[41] In *Harris*, a company president had subjected a female manager to sexual innuendo, unwanted physical touching, and insults because of her gender. After two years, she left the job.

In its decision, the Supreme Court decided that hostile environment sexual harassment need not "seriously affect psychological well-being" of the victim before Title VII is violated. According to the Court, *Meritor Savings* had adopted a "middle path" between condemning conduct that was "merely offensive" and requiring proof of "tangible psychological injury." Thus, a hostile environment is not created by the "'mere utterance of an ... epithet which engenders offensive feelings in an employee.'" On the other hand, a victim of sexual harassment need not experience a "nervous breakdown" for the law to come into play. "So long as the environment would reasonably be perceived, and is perceived, as hostile or abusive, there is no need for it also to be psychologically injurious."[42]

Harris also addressed the standard of reasonableness to be applied in judging sexual harassment claims, another issue dividing the lower federal courts. The Court opted for a two-part analysis, both components of which must be met for a violation to be found. First, the conduct must create an objectively hostile work environment — "an environment that a reasonable person would find hostile and abusive." Second, the victim must subjectively perceive the environment to be abusive. The "totality of circumstances" surrounding the alleged harassment are to guide judicial inquiry, including "the frequency of the discriminatory conduct; its severity; whether it is physically threatening or humiliating or a mere offensive utterance; and whether it unreasonably interferes with an employee's work performance."[43]

Since *Meritor Savings* and *Harris*, a broad range of hostile environment harms — frequently as concerned with lewd comments, inquiries, jokes, or displays of pornographic materials in the workplace as with overt sexual aggression — have been brought before the federal courts. *Robinson v. Jackson Shipyards, Inc.[44]* was among the first reported decisions to impose liability for sexual harassment based on the pervasive presence of sexually oriented materials—magazine foldouts or other pictorial depictions—and "sexually demeaning remarks and jokes" by male coworkers without allegations of physical assaults or sexual propositions directed at the plaintiff. Most courts, however, have limited recovery to cases involving repeated sexual demands or other offensive conduct.[45] Except for cases involving touching or extreme verbal behavior, courts are often reluctant to find that sexual derision — or claims against pornography in the workplace — is sufficient to create a hostile environment when unaccompanied by sexual demands.[46] The First Amendment has even been invoked to curb harassment claims founded solely on verbal insults or pictorial or literary matter, as impermissible content-based restrictions on free speech.[47] This tendency may be reinforced by the Court's admonition in *Oncale* that Congress never intended Title VII to become a general "code of civility." Conduct need not be overtly sexual, however, as other hostile conduct directed against the victim because of the victim's sex is also prohibited.[48] And, in line with *Meritor Savings*, evidence of a sexual harassment claimant's own provocative behavior or prior workplace conduct is generally relevant to a judicial determination of whether the defendant's conduct was unwelcome.[49]

Likewise, claims involving isolated or intermittent incidents have frequently been dismissed as insufficiently pervasive. A recurring point in the decisions is that "simple teasing, offhand comments, and isolated incidents (unless extremely serious) will not amount to discriminatory changes in the 'terms and conditions of employment.'"[50] In *Jones v. Clinton*, for example, the court ruled that considering the "totality of the circumstances," an alleged hotel incident and other encounters between Paula Jones and former President (then-Governor) Clinton were not "the kind of sustained and nontrivial conduct necessary for a claim of hostile work environment."[51] In particular, the court noted that plaintiff Jones "never missed a day of work" because of the incident nor did she complain to her supervisors; never did she seek medical or psychological treatment as a consequence of alleged harassment; and that her allegations generally failed to demonstrate any adverse workplace effects. The Seventh Circuit, in another case, concluded that while an Illinois state employee "subjectively perceived her work environment to be hostile and abusive" the paucity of sexually oriented comments complained of — three suggestive comments by a coworker over a three-month period — "were not sufficiently severe that a reasonable person would feel subjected to a hostile working environment."[52] Of course, a single incident may be actionable if it is linked to a granting or denial of an employment benefit (*quid pro quo* harassment), or if the incident involves physical assault or other exceptional circumstances.[53] The EEOC policy statement also states that the agency "will presume that the unwelcome, intentional touching of a charging party's intimate body areas is sufficiently offensive to alter the conditions of her working environment and constitute a violation of Title VII."[54]

SAME-SEX HARASSMENT

Title VII was interpreted early on by the courts and the EEOC to protect both men and women against workplace sexual harassment by the opposite sex. In *Meritor Savings,* the Court found that Congress intended "to strike at the entire spectrum of disparate treatment of men and women" in employment and read Title VII to prohibit discriminatory harassment by a supervisor "because of the subordinate's sex." Until the Supreme Court decision in *Oncale v. Sundowner Offshore Services, Inc.,* however, federal courts were sharply divided over whether the act applied when the harasser and the victim are of the same sex. Although Title VII does not prohibit direct discrimination by an employer based on an employee's sexual orientation[55] — whether homosexual, bisexual, or heterosexual — several federal appellate and trial courts found that same-sex harassment was actionable in some circumstances. In effect, "because of" sex in Title VII reached all disparate treatment based on the sex or gender of the employee, without regard to whether the harasser is male or female.[56] The Fifth Circuit, on the other hand, concluded that same-sex harassment could never form the basis of a Title VII claim.[57]

In *Oncale v. Sundowner Offshore Services, Inc.,* the U.S. Supreme Court agreed with the majority view of the federal courts that "nothing in Title VII necessarily bars a claim of discrimination 'because of ... sex' merely because the plaintiff and the defendant (or the person charged with acting on behalf of the defendant) are of the same sex."[58] The case involved *quid pro quo* and hostile environment claims of a male offshore oil rig worker who alleged that he was sexually assaulted and abused by his supervisor and two male co-workers, forcing him to quit his job. Although the Court acknowledged that Congress was "assuredly" not concerned with male-on-male sexual harassment when it enacted Title VII, it found no justification in the statutory language or the Court's precedents for excluding same-sex harassment claims from the coverage of Title VII. The opinion for the Court is notable for its emphasis on general sexual harassment principles, possibly paving the way for stricter scrutiny of sexual harassment claims in general. First, the opinion observes that federal discrimination laws do not prohibit "all verbal or physical harassment in the workplace," only conduct that is discriminatory and based on sex. Moreover, harassing or offensive conduct "is not automatically discrimination because of sex, merely because the words used have a sexual content or connotation." Instead, the Court emphasized, those alleging harassment must prove that the conduct was not just offensive, but "actually constituted" discrimination.[59] Second, reiterating *Meritor Savings* and *Harris,* only conduct so "severe or pervasive" and objectively offensive as to alter the conditions of the victim's employment is actionable so that "courts and juries do not mistake ordinary socializing in the workplace — such as male-on-male horseplay or intersexual flirtation — for discriminatory 'conditions of employment.'"[60] Another moderating aspect of the *Oncale* ruling is the Court's obvious concern for "social context" and workplace realities when appraising all sexual harassment claims — same-sex or otherwise.[61]

The full implications of *Oncale* for same sex harassment and hostile environment cases remain largely unsettled. The Court clearly reinjected the element of discrimination — "because of sex"— back into harassment law, perhaps tempering a tendency on the part of some lower courts to equate offensive behavior with a hostile environment without more. Indeed, the opinion states that "Title VII does not prohibit all verbal or physical harassment" and "requires neither asexuality or androgyny in the workplace." Because little guidance was offered, however, for determining when untoward conduct crosses the line to sex-based discrimination, lower court have been left to grapple with the issue. The Court's opinion suggests two possible approaches to demonstrating a nexus between sexually offensive conduct and gender discrimination.

> A trier of fact might reasonably find such discrimination, for example, if a female victim is harassed in such sex-specific and derogatory terms by another woman as to make it clear that the harasser is motivated by general hostility to the presence of women in the workplace. A same-sex harassment plaintiff may also, of course, offer direct comparative evidence about how the alleged harasser treated members of both sexes in a mixed-sex workplace.

It is difficult, however, to discern how either approach would aid male same-sex plaintiffs like Oncale in proving discrimination "because of sex" when they arc victims of harassment by other males on an oil rig or in other male-dominated workplaces.

The *Oncale* ruling also marked a general tempering of earlier decisions driving current trends in sexual harassment litigation. The numerous examples cited by the Court of "innocuous differences" in the way men and women interact might serve as the basis for future judicial acceptance of a wider latitude of behavior in the workplace than might otherwise have been considered permissible. The lengths to which the opinion seems to go in articulating the bounds of permissible heterosexual behavior in a same-sex harassment case reinforces this conclusion. Thus, the express approval of "intersexual flirtation" and "teasing or roughhousing" implies that a certain level of fraternization in the workplace is permissible and the consequent range of actionable conduct correspondingly reduced. In this regard, the decision's emphasis upon "social context" may complicate the already difficult judicial task of identifying a sexually hostile work environment. Does this mean, for example, that conduct permitted in a blue-collar workplace may be actionable in a white-collar, professional environment? Thus, the decision might lead to the dismissal of cases the courts have entertained in the past. At the very least, beyond its threshold endorsement of a same-sex cause of action under Title VII, the *Oncale* decision appears to raise as many questions as it answers.

Lower courts have offered answers to some of those questions. As *Oncale* emphasizes, the object of Title VII is elimination of discrimination "because of sex." Thus, inappropriate conduct that targets both sexes, or is inflicted regardless of sex, is not covered. The statute does not reach the "equal opportunity" or "bisexual" harasser who treats male and female employees the same, however inappropriately.[62] Harassment is "because of" sex only if the gender of the victim is the motivating or "but for" cause of the offensive conduct.[63] That offensive workplace conduct may be more offensive — or have a disparate impact — on female than male employees may not suffice if an intention to discriminate is lacking.[64] For example, in *Kestner v. Stanton Group, Inc.,[65]* a female employee complained about a male manager's abusive demeanor and constant yelling. Although the manager had also made several sexually suggestive and crude remarks that were gender-specific, the Sixth Circuit concluded: "That [the manager] yelled at employees, male and female, and that he cursed in front of employees, male and female, does not by itself create a hostile work environment."[66]

Similarly, the courts have generally reiterated the position that Title VII provides no remedy to a person claiming harassment at the hands of co-workers motivated solely by hostility to his perceived sexual orientation.[67] "Gender" is not to be equated with "sexual orientation" under Title VII. In *Spearman v. Ford Motor Co.,[68]* the plaintiff claimed that he had been subjected to vulgar and sexually explicit insults and graffiti by his co-workers who, he alleged, perceived him to be too feminine to fit the male image in a manufacturing plant. But because the employee's problems were found to stem from an altercation over work issues and because of his apparent homosexuality, rather than sex, the Seventh Circuit dismissed the action. If the plaintiff can show that the harassment was based on his or her failure to conform to gender stereotypes, however, an action for sexual harassment may be allowed.

The Supreme Court has denounced sexual stereotyping under Title VII in a failure to promote case,[69] and several federal appellate courts have applied the same rationale in the harassment setting. In *Nichols v. Azteca Restaurant*

Enterprizes, Inc.,[70] a male restaurant employee was addressed by his coworkers as a female and was taunted for his feminine manner of walk and serving customers, in addition to being subjected to derogatory comments based on his sexual orientation. The court ultimately found that the harassment at issue was closely linked to gender because the plaintiff's harassers discriminated against him for being too feminine.

In a subsequent case, however, the Ninth Circuit *en banc* largely disregarded sexual stereotypes, focusing instead on the "unwelcome physical conduct of a sexual nature" to permit a gay man to pursue an harassment claim. The plaintiff in *Rene v. MGM Grand Hotel[71]* was a former butler who claimed his supervisor and several fellow employees on an all male staff engaged in offensive gestures and touched his body "like they would to a woman." In this "sexual touching hostile environment" case, the appellate court ruled, the sexual orientation of the victim was "irrelevant," since "[t]he physical attacks to which Rene was subjected, which targeted body parts clearly linked to his sexuality, were 'because of ... sex.'"[72] Three judges concurred in the result, but wrote separately that the employee could sue for gender-stereotyping harassment as in *Nichols.* In both cases, they stated, a male employee was mocked for his mannerisms and addressed by coworkers in female terms "to remind [him] that he did not conform to their gender-based stereotypes."[73]

Instead of animosity or ridicule, post-*Oncale* courts have also considered issues raised by employees who are subjected to unwelcome displays of affection or sexual advances by supervisors or coworkers of the same sex. This has likewise required a judicial determination as to the motivation behind the alleged discriminatory conduct — whether based on gender or sex, which is prohibited by Title VII, or sexual orientation, which is not. In *Oncale,* the Supreme Court noted that one way by which a plaintiff can prove that an incident of same-sex harassment constitutes sex discrimination is to show that the alleged harasser made explicit or implicit proposals of sexual activity and provide "credible evidence" that the harasser was homosexual. In *Shepherd v. Slater Steels Corp.,*[74] the Seventh Circuit permitted the case to go to trial on evidence that the harasser's action was based on sexual attraction, such as repeated remarks that the plaintiff was a "handsome young man," coupled with other encounters of a sexual nature. The Fifth Circuit has decided that there are two types of evidence that are likely to be "especially [credible] proof" that the harasser may be a homosexual.[75] The first type is evidence suggesting that the harasser intended to have some kind of sexual contact with the plaintiff, rather than "merely to humiliate him for reasons unrelated to sexual interest." Second is proof that the alleged harasser made same-sex advances to others, particularly other employees.

According to the court, a harasser might make sexually demeaning remarks and putdowns for sex-neutral reasons, but it is less likely that sexual advances would be made without regard to sex. Other courts have required the plaintiff to demonstrate that the harassment was motivated by sexual desire.[76] Suffice it to say, considerable confusion persists among the lower courts as to whether gender, sexual attraction, or conduct of a sexual nature is the key factor distinguishing discrimination based on sex from sexual orientation discrimination in the same-sex harassment context. To a large extent, the answer may depend on the facts presented by the particular case.

REMEDIES

In 1991, Congress enacted amendments to the Civil Rights Act of 1964.[77] Of particular importance to sexual harassment claimants, the amendments established jury trials and compensatory and punitive damages as remedies for Title VII violations. Previously, Title VII plaintiffs had no right to a jury trial and were entitled only to equitable relief in the form of injunctions against future employer misconduct, reinstatement, and limited backpay for any loss of income resulting from any discharge, denial of promotion, or other adverse employment decision. Consequently, victims of alleged sexual harassment were often compelled to rely on state fair employment practices laws,[78] or traditional common law causes of action for assault, intentional infliction of emotional distress, unlawful interference with contract, invasion of privacy, and the like, to obtain complete monetary relief.[79] Section 102 of the 1991 amendments altered the focus of federal EEO enforcement from reliance on judicial injunctions, where voluntary conciliation efforts fail, to jury trials, and compensatory and punitive damages in Title VII actions involving intentional discrimination.[80]

Compensatory damages under the 1991 Act include "future pecuniary losses, emotional pain, suffering, inconvenience, mental anguish, loss of enjoyment of life, and other nonpecuniary losses."[81] The compensatory and punitive damages provided by §102 are "in addition to any relief authorized by Section 706(g)" of the 1964 Civil Rights Act.[82] The 1991 amendments further state that "[c]ompensatory damages award under [§ 1981a] shall not include backpay, interest on backpay, or any other type of relief authorize under section 706(g) ..." Therefore, plaintiffs may recover damages in addition to equitable relief, including backpay. Punitive damages may also be recovered against private employers where the plaintiff can demonstrate that the employer acted "with malice or reckless indifference" to the individual's federally protected rights.

Punitive damages are not recoverable, however, against a governmental entity.[83] In cases where a plaintiff seeks compensatory or punitive damages, any party may demand a jury trial.[84]

The damages remedy under the law is limited by dollar amount, however, according to the size of the defendant employer during the twenty or more calendar weeks in the current or preceding calendar year. The sum of compensatory and punitive damages awarded may not exceed: $50,000 in the case of an employer with more than 14 and fewer than 101 employees; $100,000 in the case of an employer with more than 100 and fewer than 201 employees; $200,000 in the case of an employer with more than 200 and fewer than 501 employees; and $300,000 in the case of an employer with more than 500 employees.[85] In jury trial cases, the court may not inform the jury of the damage caps set forth in the statute.

In *Pollard v. E.I. duPont de Nemours and Co.,[86]* the U.S. Supreme Court significantly expanded the amount of monetary relief that may be awarded victims of sexual harassment or other forms of intentional discrimination prohibited by Title VII. Prior to that decision, there was a dispute among the circuits as to whether "front pay" in lieu of reinstatement was authorized by § 706(g) of Title VII, or was included in "compensatory damages" and subject to the $300,000 cap imposed by the 1991 Act.[87] Front pay is money awarded for lost compensation during the period between judgment for a Title VII plaintiff and the plaintiff's reinstatement, or money awarded when reinstatement is impractical. When reinstatement is not immediately available, front pay is paid until the plaintiff is reinstated. In some instances, however, reinstatement may not be a viable option at all. Continuing hostility between the plaintiff and the employer or co-workers, or psychological injuries suffered as a result of discrimination, may prevent the plaintiff's return to the workplace. Front pay in such circumstances is a substitute for reinstatement.

The plaintiff in *Pollard* had claimed that she was a victim of co-worker harassment and that her supervisors were aware of the illegal conduct. As a consequence, she was given a medical leave of absence for psychological assistance but was later fired for refusing to return to what she claimed was a hostile work environment. At trial, Pollard was awarded $300,000 in compensatory damages – the maximum allowable – for emotional and psychological suffering but was denied any additional front pay because of the cap. The Sixth Circuit affirmed the result.

In a unanimous decision, the Supreme Court concluded that front pay is not an element of compensatory damages within the meaning of the 1991 Act, thus ruling that the statutory cap did not apply. Tracing the history of Title VII, the

Court noted that the original statute authorized backpay awards, which had been interpreted by the courts to include front pay to a date certain in the future as an alternative to reinstatement. To limit front pay to cases where there is eventual reinstatement after judgment, reasoned the Court, would leave the most egregious offenders subject to the least sanctions. Likewise, a ruling that front pay could be considered compensation for "future pecuniary losses" subject to the damages cap would fly in the face of the congressional intent behind the 1991 Act "to expand the available remedies by permitting the recovery of compensatory and punitive damages in addition to previously available remedies, such as front pay." The consequences of *Pollard* for employers may be considerable. The estimated monetary value of harassment or other intentional discrimination cases may be multiplied several times if juries or judges can be persuaded by plaintiffs' attorneys to award front pay for years, or even decades, into the future.[88]

The expansion of Title VII remedies dramatically affects the level of relief available in cases of intentional sex discrimination, where for the first time employees in the private sector have the prospect of federal compensatory and punitive damage recoveries and the right to a jury trial. The act now provides a monetary remedy for victims of sexual harassment in employment in addition to lost wages. Since harassment of the hostile environment type often occurs without economic loss to the employee, in terms of pay or otherwise, critics of the prior law charged that the sexual harassment victim was frequently without any effective federal relief. Title VII plaintiffs may now seek monetary compensation for emotional pain and suffering, and other pecuniary and nonpecuniary losses, caused by sexual harassment. Moreover, federal claims may be joined with pendent state-law claims for damages unlimited by the caps in the federal law or an election made between pursuing state and federal remedies.

LIABILITY OF EMPLOYERS AND SUPERVISORS FOR MONETARY DAMAGES

The addition of monetary damages to the arsenal of Title VII remedies rekindled inquiry into an employer's liability for harassment perpetrated by its supervisors and nonsupervisory employees and the personal liability of individual harassers. The *Ellerth* decision ratified the federal circuit courts, which had generally declared employers vicariously liable for *quid pro quo* sexual harassment committed by supervisors culminating in tangible job detriment.[89] Only those with actual authority to hire, promote, discharge, or affect the terms and conditions of employment can engage in *quid pro quo* harassment and are held to act as agents of the employer, regardless of their motivations. *Quid pro quo* harassment is viewed no differently than other forms of prohibited discrimination for which employers have routinely been held vicariously liable. Because Title VII defines employer to include "any agent" of the employer, the statute is understood to have incorporated the principle of *respondeat superior*, in effect holding "employers liable for the discriminatory [acts of] ... supervisory employees whether or not the employer knew, should have known, or approved of the supervisor's actions."[90] However, the suggestion in *Meritor Savings* that courts look to agency law in developing liability rules for hostile work environment led most lower federal courts to reject vicarious liability for employers lacking actual or constructive knowledge of environmental harassment perpetrated by a supervisor. Prior to *Ellerth* and *Faragher*, most courts made an employer liable for a hostile environment only if it knew or should have known about the harassment and failed to take prompt remedial action to end it.

Vicarious Employer Liability: The *Ellerth/Faragher* Affirmative Defense

A different set of liability principles was adopted by the Supreme Court for supervisory harassment in *Ellerth* (discussed above) and *Faragher v. City of Boca Raton*.[91] While working for the City of Boca Raton, Faragher and her female colleagues were subjected to offensive touching, comments, and gestures from two supervisors. Although Faragher did not complain to department management at the time of her employment, when she resigned from her position for reasons unrelated to the alleged harassment, Faragher sued the city under Title VII.

As in *Ellerth*, the *Faragher* Court largely abandoned the legal distinction between *quid pro quo* and hostile environment harassment, looking instead to agency principles as guides to employer liability for supervisory misconduct. The Court reiterated *Ellerth*'s determination that sexual harassment by a supervisor is not within the scope of employment. But because a supervisor is "aided" in his actions by the agency relationship, a more stringent vicarious liability standard was warranted than pertains to similar misconduct by mere co-workers, where the employer is liable for negligence only if he fails to abate conditions of which he "knew or should have known." "When a person with supervisory authority discriminates in the terms and conditions of subordinates' employment, his actions necessarily draw upon his superior position over the people who report to him, or those under them, whereas an employee generally cannot check a supervisor's abusive conduct the same way that she might deal with abuse from a co-worker."[92]

The Court also determined, however, that public policy considerations were important in crafting employer liability rules. The congressional design behind Title VII favored both the creation of anti-harassment policies and effective grievance mechanisms by employers, and a coordinate duty on the part of employees to avoid or mitigate harm. To accommodate these Title VII policies and agency principles of employers' vicarious liability, the Court in *Ellerth* and *Faragher* adopted a composite standard which for the first time explicitly allows employers an affirmative defense to liability for environmental harassment caused by supervisory misconduct. According to the Court:

> An employer is subject to vicarious liability to a victimized employee for an actionable hostile environment created by a supervisor with immediate (or successively higher) authority over the employee. When no tangible employment action is taken, a defending employer may raise an affirmative defense to liability or damages, subject to proof by a preponderance of the evidence .... The defense comprises two necessary elements: (a) that the employer exercised reasonable care to prevent and correct promptly any sexually harassing behavior, and (b) that the plaintiff employee unreasonably failed to take advantage of any preventative or corrective opportunities provided by the employer or to avoid harm otherwise. While proof that an employer had promulgated an antiharassment policy with complaint procedure is not necessary in every instance as a matter of law, the need for a stated policy suitable to the employment circumstances may appropriately be addressed in any case when litigating the first element of the defense. And while proof that an employee failed to fulfill the corresponding obligation of reasonable care to avoid harm is not limited to showing an unreasonable failure to use any complaint procedure provided by the employer, a demonstration of such failure will normally suffice to satisfy the employer's burden under the second element of the defense.[93]

The affirmative defense is unavailable, however, and employers are strictly liable for harassment of subordinate employees by their supervisors perpetrated by means of a "tangible employment action," such as discharge, demotion, or undesirable reassignment.

The affirmative defense adopted by the Court in *Ellerth* and *Faragher* imposes a duty of care on both the employer and the employees to prevent workplace harassment and to mitigate its effects. The first line of defense for the employer is to adopt and communicate to its staff and management an effective sexual harassment policy and complaint procedure. In most cases, the failure to do so — at least in the case of large employers, like the city government in *Faragher* — will result in strict liability for any harassing conduct by supervisory employees, whether or not the alleged victim suffers any adverse employment action. Questions remain, however, as to scope of that legal obligation, particularly in relation to smaller employers, since the Court's formulation appears to leave open the possibility that corrective actions short of a formalized anti-harassment policy may be reasonable, at least in some circumstances. Thus, considerations of employer size and resources, and the structure of the workplace (e.g., whether a single location or on scattered sites) may be relevant factors.

Similarly, the latest High Court decisions place the burden on aggrieved employees to avail themselves of corrective procedures provided by the employer—thereby mitigating damages caused by the alleged harassment — or risk having their claim legally barred. However, the Court did not address whether an employee's failure to take such saving action would be deemed "unreasonable" if the complainant is able to demonstrate the inadequacy of the employer's grievance procedure, if employees had suffered retaliation for invoking the procedure in the past, or if harassing supervisors previously had not been disciplined for their action. Nor do the decisions specifically address the fate of employers denied the benefit of the affirmative defense because an employee followed the complaint procedure set forth in the employer's anti-harassment policy. Is strict employer liability the rule in such cases, or is the issue to be decided in light of the overall appropriateness of the employer's remedial response? Thus, many questions remain for lower courts to decide in regard to the employer's assertion of an affirmative defense. Consequently, while clarifying the law to some extent, it may take the courts years to flesh out the concept of "reasonable care," "correct promptly," "unreasonably failed," and "tangible employment action," all key elements in the Court's definition of the employer's affirmative defense.

Some guidance may be gleaned from later federal appeals court decisions that have grappled with issues left unresolved by *Ellerth* and *Faragher.* Much judicial attention has focused on whether conduct alleged by the plaintiff amounts to a tangible employment action, nullifying the employer's affirmative defense, and to the adequacy of any corrective action taken by the employer in response to alleged harassment. Aside from hiring, discharge, promotion or demotion, and benefits decisions having direct economic consequences, an employment action may be "tangible" if it results in a significant change in employment status.[94]

In addition, most courts have read *Ellerth* to require, at a minimum, that the employer establish, disseminate, and enforce an anti-harassment policy and complaint procedure.[95] Beyond adopting an anti-harassment policy and procedures for its employees, the employer must undertake immediate and appropriate corrective action — including discipline proportionate to the seriousness of the offense — when it learns of a violation.[96] Whether the employer has responded in a prompt and reasonable manner depends on all the underlying facts and circumstances, and the harassment victim's own conduct may be a relevant factor.[97] In some cases, alleged harassers who were discharged but later exonerated have sued their employers. The employer has usually prevailed, however, as long as the decision to fire or otherwise discipline the suspected perpetrator was based on a good faith belief of misconduct after an adequate investigation was performed.[98] Even before the High Court's latest decisions, lower court rulings suggested that the most effective defensive strategy for employers to avoid liability for a hostile work environment was a proactive approach.[99] In addition, the courts have generally been reluctant to impose Title VII liability on employers who act "prophylactically" to stem harassing conditions before they begin.[100]

The practical lesson for employers is to formulate and communicate to employees a specific policy forbidding workplace harassment; to establish procedures for reporting incidents of harassment that bypass the immediate supervisor of the victim if he or she is the alleged harasser; to immediately investigate all alleged incidents and order prompt corrective action (including make-whole relief for the victim) when warranted; and to appropriately discipline the harasser.

Finally, the Court continued to build on its holdings in *Faragher* and *Ellerth* in *Kolstad v. American Dental Association*.[101] Addressing the availability of punitive damages for violations of Title VII, the Court concluded that although an employer may be vicariously liable for the misconduct of its supervisory employees, it will not be subject to punitive damages if it has made good faith efforts to comply with Title VII. The Court noted that subjecting employers that adopt antidiscrimination policies to punitive damages would undermine Title VII's objective of encouraging employers to prevent discrimination in the workplace.

Constructive Discharge

In 2004, the Supreme Court resolved a conflict among the federal circuits concerning the defenses, if any, that may be available to an employer against an employee's claim that she was forced to resign because of "intolerable" sexual harassment at the hands of a supervisor. In *Pennsylvania State Police v.*

Suders,[102] the plaintiff claimed that the tangible adverse action was supervisory harassment so severe that it drove the employee to quit, a constructive discharge in effect. The Court accepted the theory of a constructive discharge as a tangible employment action, but it also set conditions under which the employer could assert an affirmative defense and avoid strict liability under Title VII. The issue is of key importance for determining the scope of employers' vicarious liability in "supervisory" sexual harassment cases alleging a hostile work environment.

As noted, *Farager* and *Ellerth* held employers strictly liable for a sexually hostile work environment created by a supervisor, when the challenged discrimination or harassment results in a "tangible employment action." The Court defined that term categorically to mean any "significant change in employment status" that may — but not always — result in economic harm. Specifically, included were "hiring, firing, failing to promote, reassignment with significantly different responsibilities, or a decision causing a significant change in benefits"[103] However, a "constructive discharge," where the employee quits, claiming that conditions are so intolerable that he or she was effectively "fired," presented an unresolved issue. Could an employer, faced with a claim of constructive discharge, still assert the *Ellerth/Farager* defense?

The constructive discharge doctrine originated in federal labor law and was later transposed by judicial interpretation to employment discrimination cases. Basically, the courts have held that an employee alleging a constructive discharge must demonstrate the concurrence of two factors: (1) the employee suffered harassment or discrimination so intolerable that a reasonable person in the same position would have felt compelled to resign and (2) the employee's reaction to the workplace situation was reasonable given the totality of circumstances. Because of its direct economic harm on employees, the Third Circuit in *Suders* joined the Eighth Circuit,[104] concluding that constructive discharge, if proven, is the functional equivalent of an actual dismissal and amounts to a tangible employment action. Taking the opposite position, the Second and Sixth Circuits had decided that a voluntary resignation, as opposed to a dismissal, was never the kind of official action that deprived the employer of its legal defenses.[105] The opposing circuits refused to view constructive discharge as a tangible employment action because it is a "unilateral" act of the employee that is neither instigated nor ratified by the employer.

In *Suders*, the Court applied the framework of its 1998 rulings to stake out a middle ground between the conflicting approaches to constructive discharge taken by the courts of appeals. The only real difference between the harassment in *Ellerth/Farager* and this case was one of degree; that is, *Suders* presented a "worst case" scenario, or harassment "racheted up to the breaking point." But a constructive discharge claim requires more than a pattern of severe or pervasive workplace abuse as would satisfy the legal standard for ordinary harassment. Employees advancing "compound" claims must also prove that the abusive working environment became so intolerable that a reasonable person would have felt compelled to resign. Such objectively intolerable conditions could result from co-worker conduct, unofficial supervisory act, or "official" company acts. The Court's earlier decisions applied agency principles to define employer vicarious liability for a supervisor's harassment of subordinates. Only when supervisory misconduct is "aided by the agency relation," as evidenced by a tangible or "official act of the enterprise," is the employer's responsibility so obvious as to warrant strict liability. When no tangible employment action is taken, the basis for imputing blame on the employer is less evident, and the focus shifts to the Title VII policy of prevention. The employer may then defeat vicarious liability by showing that it had reasonable anti-harassment procedures in place that the employee unreasonably failed to utilize.

Ultimately, the Court held that Title VII encompasses employer liability for constructive discharge claims attributable to a supervisor, but ruled that an "employer does not have recourse to the *Ellerth/Faragher* affirmative defense when a supervisor's official act precipitates the constructive discharge; absent such a 'tangible employment action,' however, the defense is available to the employer whose supervisors are charged with harassment."[106] In recognizing hostile environment constructive discharge claims, *Suders* enhanced Title VII protection for employees who quit their jobs over intense sexual harassment by a supervisor. But the decision also makes it easier for an employer to defend against such claims by showing that it has reasonable procedures for reporting and correcting harassment of which the employee failed to avail herself. Only "if the plaintiff quits in reasonable response to an employer-sanctioned adverse action officially changing her employment status or situation, for example, a humiliating demotion, extreme cut in pay, or transfer to a position in which she would face unbearable working condition," is the employer made strictly liable for monetary damages or other Title VII relief.[107]

Moreover, even where there has been a tangible employment action, coupled with a constructive discharge or resignation, the employer may have defenses available. First, the employer may argue that the harassing conduct did not occur as alleged, or was not sufficiently severe, pervasive, or unwelcome to meet standards for a Title VII violation. Second, if the tangible employment action is shown to be unrelated to the alleged harassment, or is taken for legitimate non-discriminatory reasons – particularly, if by persons other than the alleged harasser – the employer might escape liability. Finally, the employer might be able to demonstrate that, whatever form the underlying supervisory harassment may take, it did not meet the standard for constructive discharge: "so intolerable that a reasonable person would have felt compelled to resign." But *Suders* also makes it more difficult to obtain summary judgment and avoid jury trials in sexual harassment cases involving constructive discharge claims. Under the decision, if there is any real dispute about whether the employee suffered a tangible employment action, the employer may not rely on the affirmative defense to obtain summary judgment.

Personal Liability of Harassing Supervisors and Co-Workers

Because the term "agent" is included within the definition of "employer," some division of judicial opinion initially existed regarding the personal liability of individual supervisors and co-workers for hostile environment harassment or other discriminatory conduct. However, all of the federal circuit courts to address the question eventually interpreted the term "agent" in the statutory definition as merely incorporating *respondeat superior* and refused to impose personal liability on agents.[108] These courts also note the incongruity of imposing personal liability on individuals while capping compensatory and punitive damages based on employer size, as the statute does, and exempting small businesses that employ less than 15 persons from Title VII altogether.

RETALIATION

Under Title VII, it is unlawful for employers to discriminate or retaliate against an employee "because he has opposed any practice made an unlawful employment practice [under Title VII] ... or because he has made a charge, testified, assisted, or participated in any manner in an investigation, proceeding, or hearing under [Title VII]."[109] Until recently, the scope of this retaliation provision was the subject of judicial debate. In 2006, however, the Supreme Court issued its decision in *Burlington Northern and Santa Fe Railway Co. v. White*,[110] a case that involved a plaintiff who alleged that her employer had unlawfully retaliated against her by reassigning her to a less desirable position after she had made several complaints about sexual harassment on the job.

In a 9-0 decision with one justice concurring, the Court held that the statute's retaliation provision encompasses any employer action that "would have been materially adverse to a reasonable employee or job applicant."[111] This standard, which is much broader than a standard that would have confined the retaliation provision to actions that affect only the terms and conditions of employment, generally makes it easier to sue employers if they retaliate against workers who complain about discrimination. Under the Court's interpretation, employees must establish only that the employer's actions might dissuade a worker from making a charge of discrimination. This means that an employee may successfully sue an employer for retaliation even if the employer's action does not actually result in an adverse employment action, such as being fired or losing wages.

SEXUAL HARASSMENT IN THE SCHOOLS

Title IX of the 1972 Education Amendments provides that "[no] person in the United States shall, on the basis of sex, be excluded from participation in, be denied the benefits of, or be subjected to discrimination under any education program or activity receiving Federal financial assistance,"[112] and the statute has been interpreted to provide a basis for challenging sexual harassment in classrooms and on campuses. The Court's recent decisions involving Title IX address various issues, including employer liability and the availability of damages.

Under Title IX, student victims of any form of sex discrimination, including sexual harassment, may file a written complaint with the Office of Civil Rights (OCR) for administrative determination and possible imposition of sanctions — including termination of federal funding — upon the offending educational institution.[113] In addition, school personnel who harass students may be sued individually for monetary damages and other civil remedies under 42 U.S.C. § 1983, which prohibits the deprivation of federally protected rights under "color of law."

In addition to making administrative sanctions available, Title IX provides student victims with an avenue of judicial relief. In *Cannon v. University of Chicago,[114]* the Supreme Court ruled that an implied right of action exists under Title IX for student victims of sex discrimination who need not exhaust their administrative remedies before filing suit.[115] However, the availability of monetary damages under Title IX remained uncertain until *Franklin v. Gwinnett County Public Schools.[116]* In *Franklin*, a female high school student brought an action for damages under Title IX against her school district alleging that she had been subjected to sexual harassment and abuse by a teacher. Although the harassment became known and an investigation was conducted, teachers and administrators did not act and the petitioner was subsequently discouraged from pressing charges. The Court, which found that sexual harassment by a teacher constituted discrimination on the basis of sex, held that damages were available to the sexual harassment victim if she could prove that the school district had intentionally violated Title IX.

After *Franklin*, it was clear that sexual harassment by a teacher constituted sex discrimination, but the extent to which school districts could be held liable for misconduct by its employees was less clear. The appropriate standard for measuring a school district's liability for sexual abuse of a student by a teacher remained unsettled until the Supreme Court ruling in *Gebser v. Lago Vista Independent School District*.[117] In *Gebser*, the Supreme Court answered the question of what standard of liability to apply to school districts under Title IX where a teacher harasses a student without the knowledge of school administrators. Jane Doe, a thirteen year old student, had been sexually abused by a teacher, but there was no evidence that any school official was aware of the situation until after it ended. Instead of strict liability or theory of constructive notice, Doe relied on the familiar common law principle later applied by the Court in *Ellerth* and *Faragher* that an employer is vicariously liable for an employee's injurious actions, even if committed outside the scope of employment, if the employee "was aided in accomplishing the tort by the existence of the agency relationship."[118] According to this theory, the harasser's status as a teacher made his abuse possible by placing him in an authoritative position to take advantage of his adolescent student. Because teachers are almost always "aided" by the agency relationship, however, and application of the common law rule "would generate vicarious liability in virtually every case of teacher-student harassment," the Fifth Circuit rejected the approach in favor of its actual knowledge standard.

In a 5 to 4 opinion, the Supreme Court affirmed, avoiding any comparison to the strict liability and affirmative defense framework promulgated for Title VII employment law. It held that a student who has been sexually harassed by a teacher may not recover damages against the school district "unless an official of the school district who at a minimum has authority to institute corrective measures on the district's behalf has actual knowledge of, and is deliberately indifferent to, the teacher's misconduct."[119] The differing legislative constructs of Title VII and Title IX, and an apparent reluctance to impose excessive financial liability on schools, appeared to drive the Court's decision.

Unlike Title VII, Title IX has been judicially determined to provide only an "implied" private right of action and rather than a statute of general application, it imposes legal obligations only as a condition to the receipt of federal financial assistance. These distinctions persuaded the Court to "shape a sensible remedial scheme that best comports with the statute" and its legislative history.[120] In analyzing congressional intent, the Court examined the statutory provisions for Title IX enforcement by means of federal agency termination of federal funds to noncomplying school districts following notice and opportunity to be heard. Given the express notice requirement of the statute, the majority felt it unfair to impose a vicarious or constructive notice standard on school districts in private lawsuits. Moreover, there was concern that the award of damages in any given case might unfairly exceed the amount of federal funding actually received by the school. Consequently, there was no actionable Title IX claim since responsible school administrators were without notice or "actual knowledge" of the alleged sexual relationship. The Court summarily noted that Lago Vista's failure to promulgate and publicize an anti-harassment policy and grievance procedure, as mandated by U.S. Department of Education regulations, established neither actual notice, deliberate indifference, or even discrimination under Title IX.

Davis v. Monroe County Board of Education, decided in 1999, addressed the standard of liability that should be imposed on school districts to remedy student-on-student harassment.[121] The plaintiff in *Davis* alleged that her fifth-grade daughter had been harassed by another student over a prolonged period — a fact reported to teachers on several occasions — but that school officials had failed to take corrective action. A sharply divided Court determined that the plaintiff had stated a Title IX claim. Because the statute restricts the actions of federal grant recipients, however, and not the conduct of third parties, the Court again refused to impose vicarious liability on the school district. Instead, "a recipient of federal funds may be liable in damages under Title IX only for its own misconduct."[122] School authorities' own "deliberate indifference" to student-on-student harassment could violate Title IX in certain cases. Thus, the Court held, where officials have "actual knowledge" of the harassment, where the "harasser is under the school's disciplinary authority," and where the harassment is so severe "that it can be said to deprive the victims of access to the educational opportunities or benefits provided by the school," the district may be held liable for damages under Title IX.[123]

In qualifying the *Davis* standard, the Court suggests that student harassment may be far more difficult to prove than sexual harassment in employment. Beyond requiring "actual knowledge," the Court cautioned that "schools are unlike the adult workplace" and disciplinary decisions of school administrators are not to be "second guess[ed]" by lower courts unless "clearly unreasonable" under the circumstances. Additionally, the majority emphasized that "damages are not available for simple acts of teasing and name-calling among school children, even where these comments target differences in gender."[124] In effect, *Davis* left to school administrators the task of drawing the line between innocent teasing and actionable sexual harassment — a difficult and legally perilous task at best.

In 2001, OCR revised its Title IX guidance in light of the Supreme Court's recent decisions.[125] The guidance is intended to illustrate the principles that a school should use to recognize and effectively respond to sexual harassment of students in its program.

REFERENCES

[1]   This report is based on a report that was originally prepared by Charles V. Dale, Legislative Attorney: CRS Report 98-34, *Sexual Harassment and Violence Against Women: Developments in Federal Law*, by Charles V. Dale.

[2]   Title VII prohibits employment discrimination on the basis of race, color, religion, sex, or national origin. 42 U.S.C. §§ 2000e et seq.

[3]   Title IX prohibits sex discrimination in federally funded education programs or activities. 20 U.S.C. § 1681.

[4]   42 U.S.C. § 2000e-2(a)(1).

[5]   42 U.S.C. §§ 2000e et seq.

[6]   20 U.S.C. §§ 1681 et seq. See Franklin v. Gwinnet County Pub. Sch., 503 U.S. 60 (1992).

[7]   See, e.g., Doe v. Taylor Indep. Sch. Dist., 975 F.2d 137 (5th Cir. 1992).

[8]   For more details on agency guidance on sexual harassment, see the EEOC's website at [http://www.eeoc.gov].

[9]   29 C.F.R. §1604.11(a).

[10]   Id. at § 1604.11.

[11]   Equal Employment Opportunity Commission, Policy Guidance on Current Issues of Sexual Harassment, March 19, 1990, at [http://www.eeoc.gov/ policy /docs/ currentissues.html].

[12]   Id. at 405:6695.

[13]   Id. at 405:6686.

[14]   Id.

[15]   Equal Employment Opportunity Commission, Enforcement Guidance: Vicarious Employer Liability for Unlawful Harassment by Supervisors, June 18, 1999 [http://www.eeoc.gov/policy/docs/harassment.html].

[16]   413 F. Supp. 654, 657-58 (D.D.C. 1976).

[17]   Id. at 660-61.

[18]   561 F.2d 983 (D.C.Cir. 1977).

[19] Karibian v. Columbia Univ., 14 F.3d 773, 777 (2d Cir.), cert. denied 512 U.S. 1213 (1994).

[20] 841 F.Supp 825 (N.D. Ill. 1994).

[21] 52 F.3d 543 (5th Cir. 1995).

[22] Bryson v. Chicago State Univ., 96 F.3d 912 (7th Cir. 1996). See also Durham Life Ins. Co. v. Evans, 166 F.3d 139, 153 (3d Cir. 1999).

[23] 151 F.3d 172, 175 (4th Cir. 1998).

[24] See Webb v. Cardiothoracic Surgery Assoc., 139 F.3d 532, 539 (5th Cir. 1998).

[25] Jones v. Clinton, 16 F. Supp. 2d 1054 (E.D.Ark. 1998).

[26] E.g., Cram v. Lamson and Sessions Co., 49 F.3d 466 (8th Cir. 1995); Sanders v. Casa View Baptist Church, 134 F.3d 331, 339 (5th Cir. 1998); Gary v. Long, 59 F.3d 1391, 1396 (D.C. Cir. 1995).

[27] Karibian v. Columbia Univ., supra n. 19. See also Jansen v. Packaging Corp of Am., 123 F.3d 490 (7th Cir. 1997).

[28] 524 U.S. 742 (1998).

[29] Under common law agency principles, the majority reasoned, an employer is generally immune from liability for the tortious conduct of its agent (the harassing supervisor in *Ellerth*), which is deemed to be "outside the scope of employment," unless the wrongdoer is "aided" in the harassment by "the existence of the agency relation." The "aided in the agency relation standard" differentiates supervisory harassment for which an employer may be automatically liable from similar acts committed by mere co-workers. And it is most clearly satisfied in those cases where the harassment culminates in a "tangible employment action."

[30] Ellerth, 524 U.S. 761.

[31] 641 F.2d 934 (1981).

[32] Id. at 945.

[33] 682 F.2d 897 (11th Cir. 1982). In an oft-quoted passage from its opinion, the court stated: Sexual harassment which creates a hostile or offensive environment for members of one sex is every bit the arbitrary barrier to sexual equality at the workplace that racial harassment is to racial equality. Surely, a requirement that a man or woman run a gauntlet of sexual abuse in return for the privilege of being allowed to work and make a living can be as demeaning and disconcerting as the harshest of racial epithets. A pattern of sexual harassment inflicted upon an employee because of her sex is a pattern of behavior that inflicts disparate treatment upon a member of one sex with respect to terms, conditions, or privileges of employment. There is

no requirement that an employee subjected to such disparate treatment prove in addition that she suffered tangible job detriment. Id. at 902.

[34] 477 U.S. 57 (1986).

[35] Id. at 58.

[36] Id. at 62 (quoting *Henson v. Dundee*), supra n. 33 at 904. In *Meritor Savings* the complainant alleged that her supervisor demanded sexual relations over a three-year period, fondled her in front of other employees, followed her into the women's restroom and exposed himself to her, and forcibly raped her several times. She claimed she submitted for fear of jeopardizing her employment. During the period she received several promotions which, it was undisputed, were based on merit alone so that no exchange of job advancement for sexual favors (quid pro quo harassment) was alleged or found.

[37] Id. at 68 (citing 29 C.F.R. § 1604.11(a)(1985)).

[38] Id. at 69.

[39] Id. at 72.

[40] Compare Rabidue v. Osceola Refining Co., 805 F.2d 611 (6th Cir. 1986); Scott v. Sears Roebuck, 798 F.2d 210 (7th Cir. 1986); and Brooms v. Regal Tube, 830 F.2d 1554 (11th Cir. 1987) with Andrews v. City of Philadelphia, 895 F.2d 1469 (3d Cir 1990); Burns v. McGregor Electronic Indus., Inc., 955 F.2d 559 (8th Cir. 1992); and Ellison v. Brady, 924 F.2d 872 (9th Cir. 1991).

[41] 510 U.S. 17 (1993).

[42] Id. at 21-22.

[43] Id. at 22-23.

[44] 760 F. Supp. 1486 (M.D.Fla. 1991).

[45] E.g. Highlander v. K.F.C. Nat'l Mgmt. Co., 805 F. 2d 644 (6th Cir. 1986); Waltman v. Int'l Paper Co., 875 F.2d 468, 475 (5th Cir. 1989); King v. Bd. of Regents, 898 F.2d 533, 537 (7th Cir. 1990). But cf. Vance v. Southern Tel. and Tel. Co., 863 F.2d 1503, 1510 (llth Cir. 1989).

[46] E.g. Cowan v. Prudential Ins. Co. of Am., 141 F.3d 751, 758 (7th Cir. 1998); Hall v. Gus Constr/ Co., 842 F.2d 1010, 1017 (8th Cir. 1988); Jones v. Flagship Int'l, 793 F.2d 714 (5th Cir. 1986), cert. denied, 479 U.S. 1065 (1987).

[47] E.g. DeAngelis v. El Paso Officers' Ass'n, 51 F.3d 596 (5th Cir. 1995); Johnson v. County of Los Angeles Fire Dep't, 865 F. Supp, 1430, 1440 (C.D.Cal. 1994). But cf. O'Rourke v. City of Providence, 235 F.3d at 735-36; Aguilar v. Avis Rent A Car Sys., Inc., 21 Cal. 4th 121 (1999), cert. denied, 529 U.S. 1138 (2000).

[48] See Carter v. Chrysler Corp., 173 F.3d 693, 701 (8th Cir. 1999); Andrews v.
      City of Philadelphia, 898 F.2d 1469, 1485 (3d Cir. 1990); Bell v. Crackin
      Good Bakers, Inc., 777 F.2d 1497, 1503 (11th Cir. 1985); McKinney v.
      Dole, 765 F.2d 1129, 1138 (D.C.Cir. 1985). But cf. Brown v. Henderson,
      257 F.3d 246 (2d Cir. 2001).

[49] See, e.g., Jones v. Wesco Inv. Inc., 846 F.2d 1154 n.5 (8th Cir. 1988);
      Swentek v. USAIR, Inc., 830 F.2d 552, 556 (4th Cir. 1987).

[50] Clark County Sch. Dist. v. Breeden, 532 U.S. 268 (2001). See also Scusa v.
      Nestle USA Co., 181 F.3d 958 (8th Cir. 1999); Lam v. Curators of the Univ.
      of Mo., 122 F.3d 654, 656-57 (8th Cir. 1997); Sprague v. Thorn Am., Inc,
      129 F.3d 1355, 1366 (7th Cir. 1997); Saxton v. Am. Tel. and Tel. Co., 10
      F.3d 526, 534 (7th Cir. 1993); Chamberlin v. 101 Realty, 915 F.2d 777 (lst
      Cir. 1990); Drinkwater v. Union Carbide Corp., 904 F.2d 853 (3d Cir.
      1990); Ebert v. Lamar Truck Plaza, 878 F.2d 338 (10th Cir. 1989).

[51] Jones v. Clinton, 990 F. Supp. 657, 675-76 (D. Ark. 1998).

[52] McKensie v. Illinois Dep't of Transp., 92 F.3d 473, 478 (7th Cir. 1996). See
      also Butler v. Ysleta Indep. Sch. Dist., 161 F.3d 263 (5th Cir. 1998); Penry
      v. Fed. Home Loan Bank of Topeka, 155 F.3d 1257 (10th Cir. 1998). But cf.
      Abeita v. TransAm. Mailings, 159 F.3d 246 (6th Cir. 1998).

[53] E.g. Howley v. Town of Stratford, 217 F.3d 148 (2d Cir. 2000); Davis v.
      U.S. Postal Service, 142 F.3d 1334 (10th Cir. 1998); Crisonino v. New York
      City Hous. Auth., 985 F. Supp. 385 (S.D.N.Y. 1997).

[54] Equal Employment Opportunity Commission, Policy Guidance on Current
      Issues   of   Sexual   Harassment,   March   19,   1990,   at
      [http://www.eeoc.gov/policy /docs/ currentissues.html].

[55] Ulane v. E. Airlines, Inc., 742 F.2d 1081 (7th Cir. 1984), cert. denied, 471
      U.S. 1017 (1985).

[56] See, e.g., Yeary v. Goodwill Indus.- Knoxville, Inc., 107 F.3d 443 (6th Cir.
      1997); Baskerville v. Culligan Int'l Co., 50 F.3d 428, 430 (7th Cir. 1995);
      Quick v. Donaldson Co., 90 F.3d 1372 (8th Cir. 1996).

[57] Garcia v. Elf Atochem N. Am., 28 F.3d 449 (5th Cir. 1994).

[58] 523 U.S. 75, 79 (1998).

[59] Id. at 80-81.

[60] Id. at 81.

[61] Id. at 81-82.

[62] See, e.g., Simonton v. Runyon, 232 F.3d 33 (2d Cir. 2000); Hamner v. St.
      Vincent Hosp. and Health Care Ctr., Inc., 224 F.3d 701 (7th Cir. 2000).

[63] Green v. Adm. of the Tulane Educ. Fund, 284 F.3d 642, 659 (5th Cir. 2002);
      Succar v. Dade County Sch. Bd., 229 F.3d 1343, 1345 (11th Cir. 2000).

[64] EEOC v. Nat'l Educ. Ass'n, 422 F.3d 840, 844 (9th Cir. 2005); DeClue v. Cent. Illinois Light Co., 223 F.3d 434, 437 (7th Cir. 2001).

[65] 2006 U.S. App. LEXIS 25610 (6th Cir. 2006).

[66] Id. at *7.

[67] See, e.g., Vickers v. Fairfield Med. Ctr., 453 F.3d 757, 765 (6th Cir. 2006); Kay v. Independence Blue Cross, 142 Fed. Appx. 48 (3d Cir. 2005); Higgins v. New Balance Athletic Shoe Co., 194 F.3d 252 (1st Cir. 1999).

[68] 231 F.3d 1080 (7th Cir. 2000).

[69] Price Waterhouse v. Hopkins, 490 U.S. 228 (1989).

[70] 256 F.3d 864 (9th Cir. 2001). But cf., Kay v. Independence Blue Cross, 142 Fed. Appx. 48, 51 (3d Cir. 2005).

[71] 305 F.3d 1061 (9th Cir. 2002), cert. denied, MGM Grand Hotel, LLC v. Rene, 538 U.S. 922 (U.S. 2003).

[72] Id. at 1066.

[73] Id. at 1069.

[74] 168 F.3d 998 (7th Cir. 1999).

[75] La Day v. Catalyst Tech., Inc., 302 F.3d 474 (5th Cir. 2002).

[76] Dick v. Phone Directories Co., 397 F.3d 1256, 1264 (10th Cir. 2005);

[77] Civil Rights Act of 1991, P.L. 102-166, 105 Stat. 1071.

[78] E.g., Wirig v. Kinney Shoe Corp., 448 N.W. 2d 526, 51 FEP Cases 885 (Minn. Ct.App. 1989), aff'd in part and rev'd in part on other grounds, 461 N.W.2d 374 (Minn. Sup.Ct. 1990).

[79] See, e.g., Rojo v. Kliger, 52 Cal.3d 65, 901 P.2d 373 (Cal. Sup.Ct. 1990); Baker v. Weyerhauser Co., 903 F.2d 1342 (10th Cir. 1990); Syndex Corp. V. Dean, 820 S.W.2d 869 (Tex. App. 1991).

[80] 105 Stat. 1072, 42 U.S.C. § 1981a.

[81] 42 U.S.C. § 1981a(b)(3).

[82] Id. at § 1981a(a)(1).

[83] Id. at § 1981a(b)(1).

[84] Id. at § 1981a(c).

[85] Id. at § 1981a(b)(3).

[86] 532 U.S. 843 (2001).

[87] The Sixth Circuit in *Pollard* had held front pay subject to the cap, 213 F.2d 933, while other circuits had concluded to the contrary. E.g. Pals v. Schepel Buick and GMC Truck, Inc., 220 F.3d 495 (7th Cir. 2000); EEOC v. W and O Inc., 213 U.S. 600 (11th Cir. 2000).

[88] In a precursor to *Pollard*, for example, the Ninth Circuit affirmed a jury award of $350,000 in compensatory damages and $124,010.46 back pay for lost wages to a 59-year-old woman who was forced to quit her job due to

posttraumatic stress syndrome caused by workplace harassment. Because she claimed that her age, stress, and background would foreclose a future job or career, the trial court also awarded the employee more than $600,000 in "front pay" to cover wages lost from the date of jury verdict forward for eleven years. Amtrak argued that this front pay award must be included in the $300,000 statutory cap on damages as "future pecuniary losses" specifically covered by the statute. Gotthardt v. Nat'l R.R., 191 F.3d 1148 (9th Cir. 1999).

[89] See Horn v. Duke Homes, 755 F.2d 599, 604 (7th Cir. 1985).

[90] Meritor Sav., 477 U.S. at 70-71.

[91] 524 U.S. 775 (1998).

[92] Id. at 803.

[93] Id. at 807-08.

[94] See, e.g., Murray v. Chicago Transit Auth., 252 F.3d 880 (7th Cir. 2001); Durham Life Ins. Co v. Evans, 166 F.3d 139, 153 (3d Cir. 1999); Watts v. Kroger Co., 170 F.3d 505, 510 (5th Cir. 1999); Sharp v. City of Houston, 164 F.3d 923 (5th Cir. 1999); Reinhold v. Commonwealth of Virginia, 151 F.3d 172 (4th Cir. 1998); Webb v. Cardiothoracic Surgery Assoc., 139 F.3d 532 (5th Cir. 1998).

[95] See, e.g., Durham Life Ins. Co., 166 F.3d 139, 162 (3d Cir. 1999); Sharp, 164 F.3d at 931-32; Wilson v. Tulsa Junior College, 164 F.3d 534 (10th Cir. 1998); But cf. Hall v. Bodine Elec. Co., 276 F.3d 345 (7th Cir. 2002).

[96] See Skidmore v. Precision Printing and Packaging, Inc., 188 F.3d 606 (5th Cir. 1999); Mockler v. Multnomah County, 140 F.3d 808 813 (9th Cir. 1998).

[97] See, e.g., Gawley v. Indiana Univ., 276 F.3d 301 (7th Cir. 2002); Jackson v. Arkansas Dep't of Educ., 272 F.3d 1020 (8th Cir. 2001); Indest v. Freeman Decorating, Inc., 164 F.3d 258 (5th Cir. 1999); Coates v. Sundor Brands, Inc., 164 F.3d 1361 (11th Cir. 1999); Van Zant v. KLM Royal Dutch Airlines, 80 F.3d 708, 715 (2d Cir. 1996); Steiner v. Showboat Operating Co., 25 F.3d 1459 (9th Cir. 1994), cert. denied, 513 U.S. 1082 (1995).

[98] See, e.g., Cotran v. Rollins Hudig Hall Int'l, Inc., 17 Cal. 4th 93 (1998); Morrow v. Wal-Mart Stores, Inc., 152 F.3d 559 (7th Cir. 1998); Waggoner v. City of Garland Tex., 987 F.2d 1160, 1165 (5th Cir. 1993).

[99] See, e.g., McKenzie v. Illinois Dep't of Transp., 92 F.3d 473 (7th Cir. 1996).

[100] See, e.g., Farley v. Am. Cast Iron Pipe Co., 115 F.3d 1548 (11th Cir. 1997); Gary v. Long, 59 F. 3d 1391 (D.C. Cir 1995).

[101] 527 U.S. 526 (1999).

[102] 542 U.S. 129 (2004).

[103] Ellerth, 524 U.S. at 761.

[104] Jaros v. Lodge Net Enter. Corp., 294 F.3d 960 (8th Cir. 2002).

[105] Turner v. Dowbrands, Inc., No. 99-3984, 2000 U.S. App. LEXIS 15733 (6th Cir. 2002); Caridad v. Metro-North Commuter R.R., 191 F.3d 283 (2d Cir. 1999), cert. denied, 529 U.S. 1107 (2000).

[106] Suders, 542 U.S. at 140-141.

[107] *Id.* at 209.

[108] Lissau v. S. Food Serv., 159 F.3d 177, 181 (4th Cir. 1998); Wathen v. GE, 115 F.3d 400, 405 (6th Cir. 1997); Dici v. Pennsylvania, 91 F.3d 542, 552 (3d Cir. 1996); Haynes v. Williams, 88 F.3d 898 (10th Cir. 1996); Tomka v. Seiler Corp., 66 F.3d 1295 (2d Cir. 1995); EEOC v. AIC Sec. Investigations, Ltd., 55 F.3d 1276 (7th Cir. 1995); Gary v. Long, 59 F.3d 1391 (D.C. Cir. 1995), cert. denied, 516 U.S. 1011 (1995); Grant v. Loan Star Co., 21 F.3d 649 (5th Cir. 1994), cert. denied, 513 U.S. 1015 (1994); Miller v. Maxwell's Int'l Inc., 991 F.2d 583 (9th Cir. 1993), cert. denied, 510 U.S. 1109 (1994); Busby v. City of Orlando, 931 F.2d 764 (11th Cir. 1991).

[109] 42 U.S.C. § 2000e-3(a).

[110] 126 S. Ct. 2405 (2006).

[111] *Id.* at 2408.

[112] 20 U.S.C. § 1681(a).

[113] 34 C.F.R. § 100.7(d)(1)(1995).

[114] 441 U.S. 677 (1979).

[115] A private right of action allows an individual to sue in court for violations under a statute rather than wait for a federal agency to pursue a complaint administratively.

[116] 503 U.S. 60 (1992).

[117] 524 U.S. 274 (1998).

[118] Doe v. Lago Vista Inde. Sch. Dist., 106 F.3d 1223, 1225 (5th Cir. 1997) (citing Restatement (Second) of Agency § 219(2)(d)(1958).

[119] Gebser, 524 U.S. at 277 (1998).

[120] Id. at 284.

[121] 526 U.S. 629 (1999). Prior to *Davis*, the federal appeals courts were divided between those that refused to award Title IX damages or injunctive relief against a school district for student-on-student or "peer" sexual harassment, Rowinsky v. Bryan Indep. Sch. Dist., 80 F.3d 1006 (5th Cir.), cert. denied 519 U.S. 861 (1996), Davis v. Monroe, 120 F.3d 1390 (11th Cir. 1997), and others that had applied agency principles and Title VII legal standards to hold school officials liable for failure to take reasonable steps to prevent

known hostile environment harassment by students or other third parties. Murray v. New York Univ. Coll. of Dentistry, 57 F.3d 243, 248-50 (2d Cir. 1995); Brown v. Hot, Sexy and Safer Prod., Inc., 68 F.3d 525, 540 (lst Cir. 1995), cert. denied 516 U.S. 1159 (1996); and Clyde K. v. Puyallup Sch. Dist., 35 F.3d 1396, 1402 (9th Cir. 1994).

[122] Davis, 526 U.S. at 640.

[123] Id. at 650.

[124] Id. at 652.

[125] Department of Education, Revised Sexual Harassment Guidance: Harassment of Students By School Employees, Other Students, or Third Parties, Jan. 19, 2001, at [http://www.ed.gov/about/offices/list/ocr/docs/shguide.html].

In: Sexual Discrimination and Harassment   ISBN: 978-1-60456-380-1
Editor: Rachel C. Feldman, pp. 37-59   © 2008 Nova Science Publishers, Inc.

Chapter 2

SEX DISCRIMINATION AND THE UNITED STATES SUPREME COURT: DEVELOPMENTS IN THE LAW[*]

Jody Feder

ABSTRACT

In its sex discrimination decisions, the United States Supreme Court not only has defined the applicability of the equal protection guarantees of the Constitution and the nondiscriminatory policies of federal statutes, but also has rejected the use of gender stereotypes and has continued to recognize the discriminatory effect of gender hostility in the workplace and in schools. This report focuses on recent sex discrimination challenges based on: the equal protection guarantees of the Fourteenth and Fifth Amendments; the prohibition against employment discrimination contained in Title VII of the Civil Rights Act of 1964; and the prohibition against sex discrimination in education contained in Title IX of the Education Amendments of 1972. Although this report focuses on recent legal developments in each of these areas, this report also provides historical context by discussing selected landmark sex discrimination cases.

Despite the fact that the Court's analysis of sex discrimination challenges under the Constitution differs from its analysis of sex discrimination under the two federal statutes discussed in this report, it is apparent that the Court is willing to refine its standards of review under both

---

[*] Excerpted from CRS Report RL30253, dated June 5, 2007.

schemes to accommodate the novel claims presented by these cases. The Court's decisions in cases involving Title VII and Title IX are particularly noteworthy because they illustrate the Court's recognition of sexual harassment in both the workplace and the classroom.

In its sex discrimination decisions, the United States Supreme Court not only has defined the applicability of the equal protection guarantees of the Constitution and the nondiscriminatory policies of federal statutes, but also has rejected the use of gender stereotypes and has continued to recognize the discriminatory effect of gender hostility in the workplace and in schools. This report focuses on recent sex discrimination challenges based on: the equal protection guarantees of the Fourteenth and Fifth Amendments;[1] the prohibition against employment discrimination contained in Title VII of the Civil Rights Act of 1964;[2] and the prohibition against sex discrimination in education contained in Title IX of the Education Amendments of 1972.[3] Although this report focuses on recent legal developments in each of these areas, this report also provides historical context by discussing selected landmark sex discrimination cases.

EQUAL PROTECTION CASES

Constitutional challenges that allege discrimination on the basis of sex are premised either on the equal protection guarantees of the Fourteenth Amendment or the equal protection component of the Fifth Amendment. To maintain an equal protection challenge, government action must be established; that is, it must be shown that the government, and not a private actor, has acted in a discriminatory manner. While the Fourteenth Amendment prohibits discriminatory conduct by the states, the Fifth Amendment forbids such action by the federal government.

The Fourteenth Amendment provides, in relevant part:

> No state shall make or enforce any law which shall abridge the privileges or immunities of the citizens of the United States; nor shall any State deprive any person of life, liberty, or property, without due process of law; *nor deny to any person within its jurisdiction the equal protection of the laws*.[4]

Although the Fourteenth Amendment requires equal protection, it does not preclude the classification of individuals. The Court has noted that the Constitution does not require things which are "different in fact or opinion to be treated in law as though they were the same."[5] A classification will not offend the Constitution unless it is characterized by invidious discrimination.[6] The Court has adopted three levels of review to establish the presence of invidious discrimination:

> **Strict scrutiny**: This most active form of judicial review has been applied where there is either a suspect classification, such as race, national origin, or alienage, or a burdening of a fundamental interest such as privacy or marriage. A classification will survive strict scrutiny if the government can show that it is *necessary* to achieving a *compelling* interest.[7] Generally, statutory classifications subject to strict scrutiny are invalidated.
> **Intermediate scrutiny**: This level of review is not as rigorous as strict scrutiny. A classification will survive intermediate scrutiny if it is *substantially related* to achieving an *important* government objective.[8] Sex classifications are subject to intermediate scrutiny.
> **Rational basis review**: This least active form of judicial review allows a classification to survive an equal protection challenge if the classification is *rationally related* to a *legitimate* government interest.[9] This level of review is characterized by its deference to legislative judgment. Most economic regulations are subject to rational basis review.

The Court's adoption of intermediate scrutiny for sex classifications did not occur until 1976. In *Craig v. Boren,* the Court declared unconstitutional an Oklahoma statute that prohibited the sale of "nonintoxicating" 3.2% beer to males under the age of 21 and to females under the age of 18.[10] Females between the ages of 18 and 21, however, were allowed to purchase beer. Although the Court agreed with the state's argument that the protection of public health and safety is an important government interest, it found that the gender classification employed by the statute was not substantially related to achieving that goal. The statistical evidence presented by the state to show that more 18 to 20-year-old males were arrested for drunk driving and that males between the ages of 17 and 21 were overrepresented among those injured in traffic accidents could not establish that the statute's gender classification was substantially related to ensuring public health and safety.

In establishing an intermediate level of review for sex classifications, the *Craig* Court identified what has been a common theme in sex discrimination cases under the Fourteenth Amendment: stereotypes and generalizations about the sexes.[11] In *Craig*, the Court acknowledged its previous invalidation of statutes that premised their classifications on misconceptions concerning the role of females. The Court's rejection of the use of stereotypes may be seen in many of the cases in this area.[12] The Court's more recent decisions similarly allude to the use of stereotypes and generalizations.

For example, in *J.E.B. v. Alabama*, the Court determined that the state could not use its peremptory challenges to exclude male jurors in a paternity and child support action.[13] In reaching its conclusion, the Court reviewed the historical exclusion of women from juries because of the belief that women were "too fragile and virginal to withstand the polluted courtroom atmosphere."[14] In *J.E.B.*, the Court questioned the state's generalizations of male jurors being more sympathetic to the arguments of a father in a paternity action and female jurors being more receptive to the mother. The Court maintained that state actors who exercise peremptory challenges in reliance on gender stereotypes "ratify and reinforce prejudicial views of the relative abilities of men and women."[15] The Court feared that this discriminatory use of peremptory challenges not only would raise questions about the fairness of the entire proceeding, but also would create the impression that the judicial system had acquiesced in the denial of participation by one gender.

In *U.S. v. Virginia*, the Court conducted a more searching form of intermediate scrutiny to find unconstitutional the exclusion of women from the Virginia Military Institute (VMI).[16] Although the Court reiterated that a classification must be substantially related to an important government interest, the Court also required the state to establish an "exceedingly persuasive justification" for its actions.[17]

Virginia advanced two arguments in support of VMI's exclusion of women: first, the single-sex education offered by VMI contributed to a diversity of educational approaches in Virginia; second, VMI employed a unique adversative method of training that would be destroyed if women were admitted.

After reviewing the history of Virginia's educational system, the Court concluded that VMI was not established or maintained to promote educational diversity. In fact, VMI's "historic and constant plan" was to offer a unique educational benefit to only men,[18] rather than to complement other Virginia institutions by providing a single-sex educational option. Further, the Court recognized Virginia's historic reluctance to allow women to pursue higher education. Any interest Virginia had in maintaining educational diversity seemed to be "proffered in response to litigation."[19]

In addressing Virginia's second argument, the Court expressed concern over the exclusion of women from VMI because of generalizations about their ability. While acknowledging that most women would probably not choose the adversative method, the Court maintained that some women had the will and capacity to succeed at VMI. Following *J.E.B.*, the Court cautioned state actors not to rely on overbroad generalizations to perpetuate patterns of discrimination. While the Court believed that the adversative method did promote important goals, it concluded that the exclusion of women was not substantially related to achieving those goals.

After determining that VMI's exclusion of women violated the Fourteenth Amendment, the Court reviewed the state's remedy, a separate program for women. Virginia established the Virginia Women's Institute for Leadership (VWIL) following the adverse decision of the court of appeals. Unlike VMI, VWIL did not use the adversative method because it was believed to be inappropriate for most women,[20] and VWIL lacked the faculty, facilities, and course offerings available at VMI. Because VWIL was not a comparable single-sex institution for women, the Court concluded that it was an inadequate remedy for the state's equal protection violations. VMI subsequently became coeducational.

The Court's most recent pronouncements with respect to sex discrimination both involved immigration issues. In *Miller v. Albright*, the Court considered a challenge to § 309 of the Immigration and Nationality Act.[21] The petitioner, the child of an American father and a Filipino mother, contended that § 309 imposed additional requirements for establishing American citizenship when a child is fathered by an American citizen outside of the United States.[22] For children born of a citizen mother and an alien father, citizenship is established at birth However, for children born of a citizen father and an alien mother, citizenship is not established until the father or the child takes affirmative steps to confirm their relationship by the child's eighteenth birthday. In this case, the petitioner's father did not attempt to establish his relationship with his daughter until after her eighteenth birthday. Thus, the petitioner's application for citizenship was denied.

The case produced five different opinions. While six justices agreed that the petitioner's complaint should be dismissed, they provided different reasons for this conclusion. Justices Stevens and Rehnquist contended that the petitioner's complaint lacked merit, maintaining that § 309's distinction between "illegitimate" children of U.S. citizen mothers and "illegitimate" children of U.S. citizen fathers is permissible under heightened scrutiny because it is "eminently reasonable and justified by important Government policies."[23] Justices O'Connor and Kennedy contended, however, that the distinction could withstand only rational basis review and should not satisfy the kind of heightened scrutiny Justice Stevens seemed to conduct. Setting aside the issue of § 309's constitutionality, Justices O'Connor and Kennedy believed that the petitioner lacked the standing necessary to even pursue her claim. Finally, Justices Scalia and Thomas contended that the petitioner's complaint should be dismissed because the Court lacks the power to confer citizenship. Having acknowledged that Congress has the exclusive authority to grant citizenship, Justices Scalia and Thomas believed that there was no need to address the constitutionality of § 309. Justices Ginsburg, Breyer, and Souter dissented in opinions written by Justices Ginsburg and Breyer.

In their separate opinions, Justices Stevens, O'Connor, Ginsburg, and Breyer each addressed the petitioner's argument that § 309 invokes gender stereotypes. The petitioner contended that § 309 relies on the belief that an American father "remains aloof from day-to-day child rearing duties," and will not be as close to his child.[24] Justice Stevens, however, maintained that the statute has a non-stereotypical purpose of ensuring the existence of a blood relationship between father and child. Justice Stevens recognized that the distinction is reasonable because mothers have the opportunity to establish parentage at birth, while fathers do not always have that opportunity. Further, he contended that the distinction encourages the development of a healthy relationship between the citizen father and the foreign-born child, and fosters ties between the child and the United States. Thus, § 309's additional requirements are appropriate for fathers, but unnecessary for mothers.

In their dissenting opinions, Justices Ginsburg and Breyer contended that § 309 relies on generalizations about men and women and the ties they maintain with their children. Justice Ginsburg argued that § 309's goals of assuring ties between the citizen father and the foreign-born child, and between the child and the United States can be achieved without reference to gender, while Justice Breyer argued similarly, positing a distinction between caretaker and non-caretaker parents, rather than mother and father.

In *Nguyen v. INS*, the Court considered a second challenge to § 309.[25] The facts in *Nguyen* closely resembled those in *Miller*. Nguyen, the child of a citizen father and a non-citizen mother, born out of wedlock, challenged § 309 on the grounds that its differing requirements for acquiring citizenship, based on the sex of the citizen parent, violated the Fifth Amendment's guarantee of equal protection.

A majority of the Court concluded that § 309's differing requirements were justified by two important government objectives. First, the Court found that the government has an important interest in assuring that a biological parent-child relationship exists.[26] While a mother's relationship to a child may be established at birth or from hospital records, a father may not be present at the birth and may not be included on such records. In this way, the Court maintained, fathers and mothers are not similarly situated with regard to establishing biological parenthood.[27] Thus, a "different set of rules . . . is neither surprising nor troublesome from a constitutional perspective."[28]

Second, the Court found that the government has an important government interest in ensuring that the child and the citizen parent have some demonstrated opportunity or potential to develop a relationship "that consists of the real, everyday ties that provide a connection between child and citizen parent and, in turn, the United States."[29] The opportunity for a meaningful relationship is presented to the mother at birth. However, the father is not assured of a similar opportunity. The Court concluded that § 309 ensures that an opportunity for a meaningful relationship is presented to the father before citizenship is conferred upon his child.

As a result, the Court found that § 309's differing requirements were substantially related to the important government interests. The Court noted that by linking citizenship to the child's youth, Congress promoted an opportunity for a parent-child relationship during the formative years of the child's life.[30] Alluding to its decision in *VMI*, the Court maintained that the fit between the § 309 requirements and the important government interests was "exceedingly persuasive."[31]

Like the petitioner in *Miller*, Nguyen argued that § 309 embodied a gender-based stereotype. However, the Court found that § 309 addresses an "undeniable difference in the circumstance of the parents at the time a child is born."[32] This difference is not the result of a stereotype or "a frame of mind resulting from irrational or uncritical analysis."[33] Rather, § 309 recognizes simply that at the moment of birth, the mother's knowledge of the child is established in a way not guaranteed to the unwed father.

While the Court's recent decisions involving sex and equal protection illustrate that it is concerned with the stereotyping of men and women, it is unclear whether it will continue to subject sex classifications and any related stereotypes to a traditional form of intermediate scrutiny. The Court's requirement of an "exceedingly persuasive justification" in *VMI* suggests that it may be interested in conducting a more exacting form of judicial review for sex classifications. In his *Miller* dissent, Justice Breyer emphasized the need to apply the standard established in *VMI*. However, in *Nguyen*, both the majority and the dissenting justices, in discussing an "exceeding persuasive justification," simply reiterated the traditional test that is used when applying intermediate scrutiny.[34] Thus, it is not clear whether sex classifications in future cases will be subject to a traditional form of intermediate scrutiny or some form of heightened scrutiny.

TITLE VII OF THE CIVIL RIGHTS ACT OF 1964

Title VII prohibits an employer from discriminating against any individual with respect to hiring or the terms and condition of employment because of such individual's race, color, religion, sex, or national origin.[35] Although a wide variety of Title VII sex discrimination claims have been litigated in the courts, the major Supreme Court sex discrimination cases under Title VII have primarily focused on the following issues: pregnancy discrimination, gender stereotypes, mixed motives, sexual harassment, employer liability, and retaliation. These issues, as well as a discussion of the two different types of discrimination recognized under Title VII, are described below. This report, however, does not address pay discrimination claims brought under Title VII or the Equal Pay Act. For more information on pay discrimination issues, see CRS Report RL31867, *Pay Equity Legislation in the 110th Congress*, by Jody Feder and Linda Levine.

Disparate Treatment and Disparate Impact

The Court has developed two principal models for proving claims of employment discrimination. The "disparate treatment" model focuses on an employer's intent to discriminate. Alternately, the "disparate impact" model is concerned with the adverse effects of an employer's practices on a protected class. Under disparate impact analysis, a facially neutral employment practice may violate Title VII even if there is no evidence of an employer's intent to discriminate. To succeed, a plaintiff must demonstrate that the application of a specific employment practice has had a different effect on a particular group of employees.[36]

Both disparate treatment and disparate impact analysis involve a system of evidentiary burden shifting. Both models require the plaintiff to establish a prima facie case of discrimination.[37] If such a case can be established, the burden shifts to the employer to articulate a defense for its actions. For example, the employer may produce evidence showing that its actions are justified because of the needs of its business or that otherwise discriminatory conduct satisfies a bona fide occupational qualification (BFOQ). Under § 703(e)(1) of Title VII, an employer may discriminate on the basis of "religion, sex, or national origin in those certain instances where religion, sex, or national origin is a bona fide occupational qualification reasonably necessary to the normal operation of that particular business or enterprise."[38] Ultimately, however, the plaintiff retains the burden of persuasion; that is, the plaintiff must establish that the employer's assertion of a legitimate, nondiscriminatory reason for its actions was a pretext to obscure unlawful discrimination.[39]

Pregnancy Discrimination

In recent years, the Court has addressed Title VII and sex discrimination most frequently in the context of sexual harassment. In *UAW v. Johnson Controls*, however, the Court considered whether an employer may discriminate against fertile women because of its interest in protecting potential fetuses.[40]

Johnson Controls, a battery manufacturer, implemented a policy that excluded "women who are pregnant or who are capable of bearing children" from jobs that exposed them to lead,[41] which was the primary ingredient in the manufacturing process at Johnson Controls. Although fertile women were excluded from employment, fertile men were still permitted to work.

The Court found that Johnson Controls' policy was facially discriminatory because it did not apply to the reproductive capacity of the company's male employees in the same way it applied to that of female employees. The Court's conclusion was bolstered by the Pregnancy Discrimination Act of 1978 (PDA), which provides that discrimination "on the basis of sex" for purposes of violating Title VII includes discrimination "because of or on the basis of pregnancy, childbirth, or related medical conditions."[42]

Although Johnson Controls asserted that sex was a BFOQ for protecting fetal safety, the Court maintained that discrimination on the basis of sex for safety concerns is allowed only in narrow circumstances.[43] The Court stressed that to qualify as a BFOQ, an employment practice must relate to the essence or central mission of the employer's business.[44] Because reproductive capacity does not interfere with a woman's ability to perform work related to battery manufacturing, the Court rejected Johnson Controls' BFOQ defense.

Gender Stereotypes

The Supreme Court has also ruled that employment decisions made on the basis of gender stereotypes may constitute unlawful sex discrimination. In *Price Waterhouse v. Hopkins*,[45] the plaintiff, a woman who was denied partnership in the accounting firm where she worked, was apparently rejected because of concerns about her interpersonal skills. Some of these concerns, however, appeared to reflect gender stereotypes. For example, one male partner referred to the plaintiff as "macho," and another informed her that she could improve her chances of making partner if she learned to "walk more femininely, talk more femininely, dress more femininely, wear make-up, have her hair styled, and wear jewelry."[46] Reasoning that sex stereotyping is a form of discrimination on the basis of sex, the Court found that employment decisions that result from sex stereotypes may violate Title VII.[47]

Although the decision was in part a victory for employees who have been victims of employment actions based on gender stereotypes, another aspect of the *Hopkins* ruling favored employers by requiring a lower standard of proof when employers defend their actions in mixed motive cases. In mixed-motive cases such as *Hopkins*, there are both legitimate and illegitimate reasons for an employer's adverse employment action. In such cases, the Court held that plaintiffs must present direct, rather than circumstantial, evidence that discrimination was a "motivating factor" in the adverse action and that employers could rebut that evidence by proving that they would have made the same decision even if discrimination had not been a factor. Both of these holdings made it easier for employers to defend against discrimination lawsuits by their employees.

Mixed Motives

As noted above, a mixed motive employment discrimination case is a case in which the employer has both legitimate and illegitimate reasons for taking the challenged employment action. Several years after the Supreme Court ruled in the *Hopkins* case, Congress passed Title VII amendments that partially overturned the decision. In the amendments, Congress added a provision that defined unlawful employment actions to include situations in which discrimination is "a motivating factor for any employment practice, even though other factors also motivated the practice."[48] If an employer violates this provision but establishes that it would have taken the same employment action absent the illegitimate motive, the amendments specify that courts may grant the plaintiff declaratory and injunctive relief, as well as attorneys' fees, although plaintiffs are not entitled to damages, hiring, reinstatement, or promotion.[49]

The Title VII amendments, however, did not address certain questions regarding the evidentiary burden of proof in mixed motive cases. In 2003, the Supreme Court addressed the issue, ruling in *Desert Palace v. Costa* that direct evidence of discrimination is not required in mixed-motive cases.[50] By allowing plaintiffs to present circumstantial evidence of discrimination, the decision made it easier for employees to win in mixed motive cases.

Sexual Harassment

Courts have recognized two forms of sexual harassment under Title VII. The first, quid pro quo sexual harassment, occurs when submission to unwelcome sexual advances or other conduct of a sexual nature is made a condition of an individual's employment or is otherwise used as the basis for employment decisions. The second form of harassment involves conduct that has the purpose or effect of interfering unreasonably with an individual's work performance or of creating a hostile or offensive working environment. This second form of sexual harassment, which the Court first recognized as a cognizable claim in *Meritor Sav. Bank, FSB v. Vinson*,[51] is referred to as "hostile environment" sexual harassment.

In *Harris v. Forklift Systems, Inc.*, the Court sought to define when a workplace was sufficiently "hostile" for purposes of maintaining a claim under Title VII.[52] The petitioner, a female manager at an equipment rental company, alleged that the company's president created a hostile environment by repeatedly insulting her because of her gender and making her the target of unwanted sexual innuendos.

The Court determined that an employee does not need to suffer injury to assert a hostile environment claim under Title VII: "So long as the environment would reasonably be perceived, and is perceived, as hostile or abusive. . . there is no need for it also to be psychologically injurious."[53] The Court identified four factors that should be considered to determine whether a hostile environment exists: (1) the frequency of the discriminatory conduct; (2) the severity of such conduct; (3) whether the conduct is physically threatening or humiliating; and (4) whether the conduct interferes unreasonably with an employee's work performance.[54] Although the Court recognized these factors as those to be considered in identifying a hostile environment, it emphasized that no single factor is determinative.

Same-Sex Sexual Harassment

In 1998, the Court interpreted Title VII's prohibition against discrimination "because of. . . sex" to include harassment involving a plaintiff and defendant of the same sex.[55] The petitioner in *Oncale v. Sundowner Offshore Services, Inc.* alleged that he was physically assaulted in a sexual manner and was threatened with rape by three male co-workers.[56] Two of the co-workers had supervisory authority over the petitioner.

Although the Court acknowledged that Congress was "assuredly" not concerned with male-on-male sexual harassment when it enacted Title VII, it found no justification in the statutory language or the Court's precedents for excluding same-sex harassment claims from the coverage of Title VII.[57] At the same time, the Court stated that inquiries in same-sex harassment cases require careful consideration of the social context in which particular behavior occurs and is experienced by the claimant. For example, the Court distinguished a football player being patted on the butt in a locker room from similar behavior occurring in an office. The Court contended that this kind of consideration would prevent Title VII from becoming a "general civility code" for the American workplace.[58]

Employer Liability

The Court continued its examination of hostile environment sexual harassment in two cases involving vicarious liability. In *Faragher v. City of Boca Raton*, the Court found that an employer is vicariously liable for actionable discrimination caused by a supervisor, subject to an affirmative defense that must consider the reasonableness of the employer's conduct, as well as the conduct of the employee.[59] The petitioner, a former lifeguard for the Marine Safety Section of Boca Raton's Parks and Recreation Department, alleged that she was subject to an environment characterized by lewd remarks, gender-biased speech, and uninvited and offensive touching by her former supervisors.

Recognizing that the authority conferred as a result of a supervisor's relationship with the employer allows the supervisor greater ability to act inappropriately, the Court concluded that an employer could be vicariously liable when a supervisor misuses that authority. As the Court noted, "When a person with supervisory authority discriminates in the terms and conditions of subordinates' employment, his actions necessarily draw upon his superior position over the people who report to him. . . . whereas an employee generally cannot check a supervisor's abusive conduct the same way that she might deal with abuse from a co-worker."[60]

While the Court recognized that there could be vicarious liability for the misuse of supervisory authority, it established the availability of an affirmative defense for employers. Under this affirmative defense, an employer could assert that it exercised reasonable care to prevent and correct any sexually harassing behavior or establish that the employee unreasonably failed to take advantage of any preventive or corrective opportunities provided by the employer. The Court believed that the employer's ability to assert such an affirmative defense was consistent with Title VII's objective of encouraging employers to prevent sexual harassment from occurring.[61]

After applying its new rules to the case at bar, the Court concluded that the city did not exercise reasonable care to prevent the supervisors' harassing conduct. Although the city maintained a policy against sexual harassment, it failed to disseminate that policy to beach employees. Further, the city made no attempt to monitor the conduct of the supervisors or assure employees that they could bypass harassing supervisors to register complaints.

The Court revisited the issue of vicarious liability for employers in *Burlington Industries v. Ellerth*, a companion case to *Faragher*.[62] In *Ellerth*, the Court maintained that an employer may be found vicariously liable for harassment by a supervisor even if the employee suffers no adverse, tangible job consequences.

The petitioner in *Ellerth* alleged that she was subjected to repeated offensive remarks and gestures by a mid-level manager who supervised the petitioner's immediate supervisor. On three occasions, the manager made remarks that could be construed as threats to deny the petitioner job benefits. For example, the manager encouraged the petitioner to "loosen up" because he "could make [her] life very hard or very easy at Burlington."[63] Although Burlington maintained a policy against sexual harassment, the petitioner did not inform anyone in authority about the manager's misconduct. Instead, the petitioner resigned from her position, providing reasons unrelated to the harassment. Three weeks after her resignation, the petitioner informed Burlington of her true reasons for leaving.

While the manager's threats suggested that the claim should be analyzed as a quid pro quo claim, the Court categorized it as a hostile environment claim because it involved only unfulfilled threats. After reviewing the petitioner's claim in terms similar to *Faragher*, the Court determined that the manager at Burlington also misused his supervisory authority. The Court concluded that Burlington should be given the opportunity to assert and prove an affirmative defense to liability.

The Court has also addressed the availability of punitive damages for violations of Title VII. In *Kolstad v. American Dental Association*,[64] the Court continued to build on its holdings in *Faragher* and *Ellerth* by concluding that although an employer may be vicariously liable for the misconduct of its supervisory employees, it will not be subject to punitive damages if it has made good faith efforts to comply with Title VII. The Court noted that subjecting employers that adopt antidiscrimination policies to punitive damages would undermine Title VII's objective of encouraging employers to prevent discrimination in the workplace.

In 2004 the Supreme Court considered the defenses, if any, that may be available to an employer against an employee's claim that she was forced to resign because of "intolerable" sexual harassment at the hands of a supervisor. As noted above, an employer may generally assert an affirmative defense to supervisory harassment under the Court's 1998 rulings in *Faragher* and *Ellerth*. The defense is not available, however, if the harassment includes a "tangible employment action,"such as discharge or demotion. In *Pennsylvania State Police v. Suders*,[65] the plaintiff claimed the tangible adverse action was supervisory harassment so severe that it drove the employee to quit, a constructive discharge in effect. The Court, in an opinion by Justice Ginsburg, only Justice Thomas dissenting, accepted the theory of a constructive discharge as a tangible employment action, but it also set conditions under which the employer could assert an affirmative defense and avoid strict liability under Title VII of the 1964 Civil Rights Act.[66] The issue was key to determining the scope of employers' vicarious liability in "supervisory" sexual harassment cases alleging a hostile work environment.

In *Faragher* and *Ellerth* , the Court had sought to clarify the nature and scope of an employer's legal liability for the discriminatory and harassing conduct of its supervisors in Title VII cases. It held employers strictly liable for a sexually hostile work environment created by a supervisor, when the challenged discrimination or harassment results in a "tangible employment action."[67] But in the absence of such a "company act" the employer may raise an affirmative defense based on its having in place a reasonable remedial process and on the employee's failure to take advantage of it. Thus, the *Ellerth/Faragher* defense has two components: "(a) that the employer exercised reasonable care to prevent and correct promptly any sexually harassing behavior, and (b) that the plaintiff employee unreasonably failed to take advantage of any preventative or corrective opportunities provided by the employer or to avoid harm otherwise."[68]

The Supreme Court defined a "tangible employment action" categorically to mean any "significant change in employment status," that may — but not always —result in economic harm. Specifically, the term includes "hiring, firing, failing to promote, reassignment with significantly different responsibilities, or a decision causing a significant change in benefits"[69] However, a "constructive discharge," where the employee quits, claiming that conditions are so intolerable that he or she was effectively "fired," presented an unresolved issue. Could an employer, faced with a claim of constructive discharge, still assert the *Ellerth/Faragher* defense?

Ultimately, the Court held that Title VII encompasses employer liability for constructive discharge claims attributable to a supervisor, but ruled that an "employer does not have recourse to the *Ellerth/Faragher* affirmative defense when a supervisor's official act precipitates the constructive discharge; absent such a 'tangible employment action,' however, the defense is available to the employer whose supervisors are charged with harassment."[70] In recognizing hostile environment constructive discharge claims, *Suders* enhanced Title VII protection for employees who quit their jobs over intense sexual harassment by a supervisor. But the decision also makes it easier for an employer to defend against such claims by showing that it has reasonable procedures for reporting and correcting harassment of which the employee failed to avail herself. Only "if the plaintiff quits in reasonable response to an employer-sanctioned adverse action officially changing her employment status or situation, for example, a humiliating demotion, extreme cut in pay, or transfer to a position in which she would face unbearable working condition," is the employer made strictly liable for monetary damages or other Title VII relief.[71]

Moreover, even where there has been a tangible employment action, coupled with a constructive discharge or resignation, the employer may have defenses available. First, the employer may argue that the harassing conduct did not occur as alleged, or was not sufficiently severe, pervasive, or unwelcome to meet standards for a Title VII violation. Second, if the tangible employment action is shown to be unrelated to the alleged harassment, or is taken for legitimate non-discriminatory reasons — particularly, if by persons other than the alleged harasser — the employer might escape liability. Finally, the employer might be able to demonstrate that, whatever form the underlying supervisory harassment may take, it did not meet the standard for constructive discharge: "so intolerable that a reasonable person would have felt compelled to resign." But *Suders* also makes it more difficult to obtain summary judgment and avoid jury trials in sexual harassment cases involving constructive discharge claims. Under the decision, if there is any real dispute about whether the employee suffered a tangible employment action, the employer may not rely on the affirmative defense to obtain summary judgment.

Retaliation

In 2006, the Supreme Court issued its decision in *Burlington Northern and Santa Fe Railway Co. v. White*,[72] a case that involved questions about the scope of the retaliation provision under Title VII. In a 9-0 decision with one justice concurring, the Court held that the statute's retaliation provision encompasses any employer action that "would have been materially adverse to a reasonable employee or job applicant."[73] This standard, which is much broader than a standard that would have confined the retaliation provision to actions that affect only the terms and conditions of employment, generally makes it easier to sue employers if they retaliate against workers who complain about discrimination. Under the Court's interpretation, employees must establish only that the employer's actions might dissuade a worker from making a charge of discrimination. This means that an employee may successfully sue an employer for retaliation even if the employer's action does not actually result in an adverse employment action, such as being fired or losing wages.

TITLE IX OF THE EDUCATION AMENDMENTS OF 1972

Title IX of the Education Amendments of 1972 prohibits discrimination on the basis of sex in educational programs and activities that receive federal funding. Until recently, Title IX claims have been most common among women and girls challenging inequities in sports programs,[74] but Title IX also provides a basis for challenging sexual harassment in classrooms and on campuses.

Title IX provides, in relevant part, that "[n]o person in the United States shall, on the basis of sex, be excluded from participation in, be denied the benefits of, or be subjected to discrimination under any education program or activity receiving Federal financial assistance...."[75] The Court's recent decisions involving Title IX address various issues, including the availability of damages, the parties that are subject to liability, and the scope of retaliation claims.

In an early Title IX case, the Supreme Court held that the statute provides student victims with an avenue of judicial relief. In *Cannon v. University of Chicago*,[76] the Court ruled that an implied right of action exists under Title IX for student victims of sex discrimination who need not exhaust their administrative remedies before filing suit. However, the availability of monetary damages under Title IX remained uncertain until *Franklin v. Gwinnett County Public Schools*.[77] In *Franklin*, a female high school student brought an action for damages under Title IX against her school district alleging that she had been subjected to sexual harassment and abuse by a teacher. Although the harassment became known and an investigation was conducted, teachers and administrators did not act and the petitioner was subsequently discouraged from pressing charges. The Court, which found that sexual harassment by a teacher constituted discrimination on the basis of sex, held that damages were available to the sexual harassment victim if she could prove that the school district had intentionally violated Title IX.

After *Franklin*, it was clear that sexual harassment by a teacher constituted sex discrimination, but the extent to which school districts could be held liable for misconduct by its employees was less clear. The appropriate standard for measuring a school district's liability for sexual abuse of a student by a teacher remained unsettled until the Supreme Court ruling in *Gebser v. Lago Vista Independent School District*.[78] In *Gebser*, the Court determined that a school district will not be held liable under Title IX for a teacher's sexual harassment of a student if the school district did not have actual notice of the harassment and did not exhibit deliberate indifference to the misconduct.[79] The petitioner, a female high school student, was involved in a sexual relationship with one of her teachers. Unlike the situation in *Franklin*, the school district did not have actual notice of any sexual relationship between the petitioner and the teacher until they were discovered by a police officer. The principal of the petitioner's school did learn of inappropriate comments made by the teacher prior to the discovery, but he cautioned the teacher about such comments. After the sexual relationship became known, the school district quickly terminated the teacher. Despite the school district's actions, the petitioner argued that the school district should be found liable on the basis of vicarious liability or constructive notice.[80]

In requiring the school district to have actual notice of the harassment, the Court discussed the absence of an express cause of action under Title IX. Unlike Title VII, Title IX does not address damages or the particular situations in which damages are available.[81] While Title IX does address a denial of funds for noncompliance with its provisions, it does not provide for a private right of action. Instead, a private right of action has been judicially implied.[82]

Because Title IX does not contain any reference to the recovery of damages in private actions, the Court reasoned that its recognition of theories of vicarious liability and constructive notice would allow an unlimited recovery where Congress has not spoken.[83] Stated differently, the Court was reluctant to expand the availability of damages for such theories when Title IX failed to provide initially for a private cause of action. In this way, the Court sought to refine its holding in *Franklin* and limit those situations in which a remedy for damages would lie.

The Court believed that Title IX's remedial scheme would be undermined if it did not require that a school district have actual notice of a teacher's sexual harassment. Under Title IX, financial assistance will not be denied until the "appropriate person or persons" have been advised of the discrimination and have failed to end the discrimination voluntarily.[84] An "appropriate person" is an official of the entity receiving funds who has the authority to take corrective action.[85] Because the school district in *Gebser* did not have actual notice of the sexual relationship, it could not have taken any steps to end the alleged discrimination.

In addition, the Court stated that damages will not be available unless it is shown that a response exhibits a deliberate indifference to the discrimination; that is, there must be "an official decision by the recipient not to remedy the violation."[86] In *Gebser*, the school district responded to the situation by first cautioning the teacher, and then terminating him once the relationship was discovered. Thus, the Court concluded that the school district did not act with deliberate indifference.

Davis v. Monroe County Board of Education, decided in 1999, addressed the standard of liability that should be imposed on school districts to remedy student-on-student harassment.[87] The plaintiff in *Davis* alleged that her fifth-grade daughter had been harassed by another student over a prolonged period — a fact reported to teachers on several occasions — but that school officials had failed to take corrective action. Justice O'Connor, writing for a sharply divided court, determined that the plaintiff had stated a Title IX claim. Because the statute restricts the actions of federal grant recipients, however, and not the conduct of third parties, the Court again refused to impose vicarious liability on the school district. Instead, "a recipient of federal funds may be liable in damages under Title IX only for its own misconduct."[88] School authorities' own "deliberate indifference" to student-on-student harassment could violate Title IX in certain cases. Thus, the Court held, where officials have "actual knowledge" of the harassment, where the "harasser is under the school's disciplinary authority," and where the harassment is so severe "that it can be said to deprive the victims of access to the educational opportunities or benefits provided by the school," the district may be held liable for damages under Title IX.[89]

While the development of sex discrimination law under Title IX owes much to Title VII, the *Davis* Court's recognition of student-on-student harassment highlights dramatic differences between the two statutes. Indeed, in qualifying the *Davis* standard, the Court suggested that student harassment may be far more difficult to prove than sexual harassment in employment. Beyond requiring "actual knowledge," Justice O'Connor cautioned that "schools are unlike adult workplaces" and disciplinary decisions of school administrators are not to be "second guess[ed]" by lower courts unless "clearly unreasonable" under the circumstances. Additionally, the majority emphasized that "damages are not available for simple acts of teasing and name-calling among school children, even where these comments target differences in gender."[90] In effect, *Davis* left to school administrators the task of drawing the line between innocent teasing and actionable sexual harassment — a difficult and legally perilous task at best.

In a separate decision the same year, the Court found that a private organization is not subject to Title IX simply because it receives payments from entities that receive federal financial assistance. In *National Collegiate Athletic Association v. Smith*,[91] the respondent, a female graduate student, alleged that the National Collegiate Athletic Association (NCAA) discriminated against her on the basis of sex by denying her permission to play intercollegiate volleyball at two federally assisted institutions. Under NCAA rules, a graduate student is permitted to participate in intercollegiate athletics only at the institution that awarded her undergraduate degree. The respondent, who was enrolled at two different universities for her graduate degree, argued that the NCAA granted more waivers from eligibility restrictions to male graduate students than to female graduate students.

The Court concluded that the NCAA was not a recipient of Title IX funds because the NCAA did not receive federal assistance either directly or through an intermediary. Instead, it received dues payments from member institutions. The Court stated, "[a]t most, the Association's receipt of dues demonstrates that it indirectly benefits from the federal assistance afforded its members. This showing, without more, is insufficient to trigger Title IX coverage."[92] Because the Court found that the NCAA was not amenable to suit, it did not address the respondent's substantive allegations of discrimination.

More recently, the Court handed down its decision in *Jackson v. Birmingham Board of Education*.[93] In this case, which involved a girl's basketball coach who claimed that he was removed from his coaching position in retaliation for his complaints about unequal treatment of the girl's team, the Court held that Title IX not only encompasses retaliation claims, but also is available to individuals who complain about sex discrimination, even if such individuals themselves are not the direct victims of sex discrimination.[94] Reasoning that "Title IX's enforcement scheme would unravel" "if retaliation were not prohibited,"[95] the Court concluded that "when a funding recipient retaliates against a person because he complains of sex discrimination, this constitutes intentional discrimination on the basis of sex in violation of Title IX."[96]

REFERENCES

[1]   U.S. Const. amend. V; U.S. Const. amend. XIV, § 1.

[2]   42 U.S.C. §§ 2000e et seq.

[3]   20 U.S.C. §§ 1681 et seq.

[4]   U.S. Const. amend. XIV, § 1 (emphasis added).

[5]   Tigner v. Texas, 310 U.S. 141, 147 (1940).

[6]   *See* Ferguson v. Skrupa, 372 U.S. 726, 732 (1963).

[7]   *See* San Antonio Independent School District v. Rodriquez, 411 U.S. 1 (1973).

[8]   *See* Craig v. Boren, 429 U.S. 190, 197 (1976). In *U.S. v. Virginia*, the Court required the State of Virginia to provide an "exceedingly persuasive justification" for its policy of maintaining an all-male military academy. 518 U.S. 515 (1996). It is unclear whether this standard differs from the intermediate scrutiny standard of review. *See infra* text accompanying notes 16-34.

[9]   *See* Lindsley v. National Carbonic Gas Co., 220 U.S. 61 (1911); Royster Guano Co. v. Virginia, 253 U.S. 412 (1920); San Antonio School District v. Rodriguez, 411 U.S. 1 (1973); Mass Bd. of Retirement v. Murgia, 427 U.S. 307 (1976); Maher v. Roe, 432 U.S. 464 (1977).

[10]   429 U.S. 190 (1976).

[11]   *Id.* at 198.

[12]   *See, e.g.*, Califano v. Goldfarb, 430 U.S. 199 (1977) (invalidating section of the Social Security Act that permitted survivors' benefits for male widows only if they were receiving half of their support from their wives); Orr v. Orr, 440 U.S. 268 (1979) (invalidating Alabama statute that imposed alimony obligations on husbands, but not wives); Caban v. Mohammed, 441 U.S. 380 (1979) (invalidating New York statute that required the consent of the mother, but not the father, to permit the adoption of an illegitimate child); Mississippi University for Women v. Hogan, 458 U.S. 718 (1982) (invalidating policy of a state-supported university that limited admission to its nursing school to women on the grounds that it reinforced traditional stereotypes).

[13]   511 U.S. 127 (1994).

[14]   *Id.* at 133.

[15]   *Id.* at 141.

[16]   518 U.S. 515 (1996).

[17]   Id.

[18]   *Id.* at 540.

[19] *Id.* at 533.

[20] *Id.* at 549.

[21] 523 U.S. 420 (1998).

[22] 8 U.S.C. § 1409.

[23] Miller, 523 U.S. at 441.

[24] *Id.* at 443.

[25] 533 U.S. 53 (2001).

[26] *Id.* at 62.

[27] *Id.* at 63.

[28] Id.

[29] *Id.* at 65.

[30] *Id.* at 68-69.

[31] *Id.* at 70.

[32] *Id.* at 68.

[33] Id.

[34] *See, e.g., id.* at 70 ("We have explained that an 'exceedingly persuasive justification' is established 'by showing at least that the classification serves 'important governmental objectives and that the discriminatory means employed' are 'substantially related to the achievement of those objectives.'"); *id.* at 74 ("Because the Immigration and Naturalization Service (INS) has not shown an exceedingly persuasive justification for the sex based classification embodied in 8 U.S.C. § 1409(a)(4) — i.e., because it has failed to establish at least that the classification substantially relates to the achievement of important governmental objectives — I would reverse the judgment of the Court of Appeals.").

[35] Title VII provides, in relevant part, that it is an unlawful employment practice for an employer "to fail or refuse to hire or to discharge any individual, or otherwise to discriminate against any individual with respect to his compensation, terms, conditions, or privileges of employment, because of such individual's race, color, religion, sex, or national origin; or to limit, segregate, or classify his employees or applicants for employment in any way which would deprive or tend to deprive any individual of employment opportunities or otherwise adversely affect his status as an employee, because of such individual's race, color, religion, sex, or national origin." 42 U.S.C. § 2000e-2.

[36] *See* Griggs v. Duke Power Co., 401 U.S. 424 (1971).

[37] A prima facie case is a case that contains elements that are sufficient to establish a claim unless disproved.

[38] 42 U.S.C. § 2000e-2(e)(1).

[39] McDonnell Douglas Corp. v. Green, 411 U.S. 792 (U.S. 1973).

[40] 499 U.S. 187 (1991).

[41] *Id.* at 192.

[42] 42 U.S.C. § 2000e(k).

[43] Johnson Controls, 499 U.S. at 202.

[44] *See, e.g.*, Dothard v. Rawlinson, 433 U.S. 321 (1977) (finding sex to be a
      BFOQ because the employment of a female guard in a maximum-security
      male penitentiary could create a risk of violence and jeopardize the safety of
      inmates); Western Airlines, Inc. v. Criswell, 472 U.S. 400 (1985) (finding
      age to be a BFOQ in an ADEA case because the employment of an older
      flight engineer could cause a safety emergency and jeopardize the safety of
      passengers).

[45] 490 U.S. 228 (U.S. 1989).

[46] *Id.* at 234-35.

[47] *Id.* at 250-51.

[48] 42 U.S.C. § 2000e-2(m).

[49] *Id.* at § 2000e-5(g)(2).

[50] Desert Palace, Inc. v. Costa, 539 U.S. 90 (U.S. 2003).

[51] 477 U.S. 57 (U.S. 1986).

[52] 510 U.S. 17 (1993).

[53] *Id.* at 22.

[54] *Id.* at 23.

[55] 42 U.S.C. § 2000e-2.

[56] 523 U.S. 75, 77 (1998).

[57] *Id.* at 79.

[58] *Id.* at 80.

[59] 524 U.S. 775 (1998).

[60] *Id.* at 803.

[61] *Id.* at 805.

[62] 524 U.S. 742 (1998).

[63] *Id.* at 748.

[64] 527 U.S. 526 (1999).

[65] 542 U.S. 129 (2004).

[66] 42 U.S.C. §§ 2000e et seq.

[67] 524 U.S. 742, 765 (1998); 524 U.S. 775, 807 (1998).

[68] Pa. State Police v. Suders, 542 U.S. 129, 137-38 (2004).

[69] Ellerth, 524 U.S. at 761.

[70] Suders, 542 U.S. at 140-141.

[71] *Id.* at 209.

[72]   126 S. Ct. 2405 (2006).

[73]   *Id.* at 2408.

[74]   See CRS Report RL31709, Title IX, Sex Discrimination, and Intercollegiate Athletics: A Legal Overview, by Jody Feder.

[75]   20 U.S.C. § 1681(a).

[76]   441 U.S. 677 (1979).

[77]   503 U.S. 60 (1992).

[78]   524 U.S. 274 (1998).

[79]   Id.

[80]   Under a theory of constructive notice, liability would be established on the grounds that the school district knew or should have known about the harassment, but failed to discover and eliminate it.

[81]   Gebser, 24 U.S. at 283-84.

[82]   *See* Cannon v. University of Chicago, 441 U.S. 677 (1979). A private right of action allows an individual to sue in court for violations under a statute rather than wait for a federal agency to pursue a complaint administratively.

[83]   Gebser, 524 U.S. at 286.

[84]   20 U.S.C. § 1682.

[85]   Gebser, 524 U.S. at 290.

[86]   Id.

[87]   526 U.S. 629 (U.S. 1999).

[88]   *Id.* at 640.

[89]   *Id.* at 650.

[90]   *Id.* at 648-52.

[91]   525 U.S. 459 (1999).

[92]   *Id.* at 468.

[93]   544 U.S. 167 (2005).

[94]   *Id.* at 171.

[95]   *Id.* at 180.

[96]   *Id.* at 174 (internal quotations omitted).

In: Sexual Discrimination and Harassment   ISBN: 978-1-60456-380-1
Editor: Rachel C. Feldman, pp. 61-77   © 2008 Nova Science Publishers, Inc.

Chapter 3

THE CONVENTION ON THE ELIMINATION OF ALL FORMS OF DISCRIMINATION AGAINST WOMEN (CEDAW): CONGRESSIONAL ISSUES[*]

Luisa Blanchfield

ABSTRACT

The U.N. Convention on the Elimination of All Forms of Discrimination Against Women calls for Parties to eliminate discrimination against women in all areas of life, including healthcare, education, employment, domestic relations, law, commercial transactions, and political participation. As of November 2, 2006, the Convention was ratified or acceded to by 185 countries.

President Jimmy Carter submitted the Convention to the Senate in 1980. The Senate Foreign Relations Committee held hearings on the Convention in 1988, 1990, 1994, and 2002, but the treaty was never considered for ratification by the full Senate. The George W. Bush Administration began conducting a full legal and policy review of the Convention in 2002. On February 7, 2007, the Administration transmitted a letter to the Senate Foreign Relations Committee stating that it does not support Senate action on the treaty at this time.

U.S. ratification of CEDAW is a contentious policy issue that has generated considerable debate in Congress and among the general public. Supporters of U.S. ratification contend that the Convention is a valuable

---

[*] Excerpted from CRS Report RL33652, dated April 5, 2007.

mechanism for fighting women's discrimination worldwide. They argue that U.S. ratification of the treaty will give the Convention additional legitimacy, and that it will further empower women who fight discrimination in other countries. Opponents of ratification contend that the Convention is not the best or most efficient way to eliminate discrimination against women. They believe ratification will undermine U.S. sovereignty and impact U.S. social policy related to family planning and abortion.

This report provides background on CEDAW developments, including U.S. policy and congressional actions, and considers arguments for and against ratification.

CEDAW BACKGROUND AND STRUCTURE

Current Status

The Convention on the Elimination of All Forms of Discrimination Against Women (CEDAW or the Convention) is the only comprehensive international U.N. treaty that specifically focuses on the rights of women.[1] As of November 2, 2006, the Convention was ratified or acceded to by 185 countries. Some States Parties[2] have filed reservations with sections of the Convention that do not align with their existing religious or national laws, and in some cases countries have objected to the reservations of other countries.[3] The United States is the only country to have signed but not ratified the Convention.[4]

Mandate

The Convention requires States Parties to work towards eliminating discrimination against women in all areas of life. This includes equality in legal status, political participation, employment, education, healthcare, and the family structure.[5] Article 2 of the Convention specifies that States Parties should undertake to "embody the principle of equality of men and women in their national constitutions or other appropriate legislation... to ensure, through law and other appropriate means, the practical realization of this principle." The Convention defines discrimination against women as

> any distinction, exclusion or restriction made on the basis of sex which has the effect or purpose of impairing or nullifying the recognition, enjoyment or exercise by women irrespective of their marital status, on a

basis of equality of men and women, of human rights and fundamental freedoms in the political, economic, social, cultural, civil, or any other field.

The Convention specifically calls for the suppression of female trafficking, equal pay with men, more attention to the equality of rural women, and the freedom to choose a marriage partner, among other things.

On October 6, 1999, the U.N. General Assembly adopted an Optional Protocol to strengthen the Convention.[6] The Protocol entered into force on December 22, 2000, and has been ratified by 84 countries. The Protocol includes a "communications procedure" that allows groups or individuals to file complaints with the CEDAW Committee. It also incorporates an "inquiry procedure" that allows the Committee to explore potential abuses of women's rights in countries that are party to the Protocol.

Evolution of the Convention

The United Nations adopted several treaties addressing specific aspects of women's rights prior to adoption of CEDAW in 1979, including the Convention on the Political Rights of Women (1952), and the Convention on the Consent to Marriage (1957).[7] In 1967, after two years of negotiations, the U.N. General Assembly adopted the Declaration on the Elimination of Discrimination Against Women, a non-binding document that laid the groundwork for CEDAW. Subsequently, the U.N. Commission on the Status of Women drafted CEDAW, which the General Assembly adopted on December 19, 1979.[8] The Convention entered into force on September 3, 1981, after receiving the required 20 ratifications.

THE COMMITTEE ON THE ELIMINATION OF DISCRIMINATION AGAINST WOMEN

The Committee on the Elimination of Discrimination Against Women (the Committee) was established in 1982 under Article 17 of the Convention as a mechanism to monitor the progress of implementation.[9] It is composed of 23 independent experts who are elected at a meeting of States Parties to the Convention by secret ballot, with consideration given to the principle of equitable geographic distribution.[10] Each State Party may nominate one expert and, if elected, the expert serves a four-year term. The majority of the Committee experts are women who, according to the Convention, should have "high moral standing and competence," and "represent different forms of civilization as well as principal legal systems." The Committee is led by a Chairperson, three Vice Chairpersons, and a rapporteur elected by the States Parties. The Chairperson directs the discussion and decision-making process and represents the Convention at international conferences and events. The Committee reports annually on its activities to the U.N. General Assembly through the Economic and Social Council, and meets twice a year at U.N. Headquarters in New York.[11]

The Committee is responsible for reviewing the reports on national CEDAW implementation submitted by States Parties. Countries are required to submit an initial report within the first year of ratification or accession, followed by a report every four years. The reports identify areas of progress as well as concerns or difficulties with implementation. The Committee engages in an open dialogue and exchange of ideas with the reporting country and compiles recommendations and conclusions based on its findings, which include general recommendations on crosscutting issues of concern. The Committee has made over 25 recommendations since 1986, covering a wide range of women's issues such as improvement in education and public information programs, elimination of female circumcision, equality in marriage and family relations, and violence against women.[12]

The 37th session of the CEDAW Committee was held from January 15 to February 2, 2007. The Committee reviewed the reports of 15 countries.[13] It urged India to remove some its treaty reservations involving stereotypes, family life, and marriage. It also recommended that Tajikistan take "practical measures," such as implementing quota policies, to improve women's political participation. The Committee also considered reports on CEDAW implementation in the U.N. specialized agencies, including the U.N. Educational, Scientific, and Cultural Organization (UNESCO), and the Food and Agriculture Organization (FAO).[14]

The next CEDAW Committee session will be held in New York from May 14 to June 1, 2007. The Committee is scheduled to consider initial reports from Mauritania, Mozambique, Niger, Pakistan, Serbia, Sierra Leone, Syrian Arab Republic, and Vanuatu.

U.S. POLICY

Administration Actions

Successive U.S. Administrations have strongly supported the Convention's overall goal of eliminating discrimination against women. They have disagreed, however, on whether the Convention is the most efficient and appropriate means of achieving this goal. President Jimmy Carter signed the Convention on July 17, 1980, and transmitted it to the Senate for advice and consent on November 12 of the same year. The Reagan and first Bush Administrations did not support ratification and the Convention remained pending in the Senate Committee on Foreign Relations. The Clinton Administration supported ratification, and in 1994 submitted a treaty package to the Senate for advice and consent to ratification. The package included nine proposed "conditions," or "RUDs" to the Convention, including four reservations, three understandings, and two declarations.[15] The Foreign Relations Committee reported the Convention favorably, but it never came to vote in the full Senate. The reservations recommended by the Clinton Administration addressed the following issues:

- "private conduct," which made clear that the United States "does not accept any obligation under the Convention to regulate private conduct except as mandated by the Constitution and U.S. law";
- "combat assignments," which stated that the United States "does not accept an obligation under the Convention to put women in all combat positions";
- "comparable worth," which made clear that the United States would not accept the doctrine of comparable worth based on the Convention's broad description; and
- "paid maternity leave," which stated that the United States could not guarantee paid maternity leave as the Convention stipulates because it is not a requirement under U.S. federal or state law.

The three understandings submitted by the Clinton Administration stated that 1) the United States will fulfill its obligations under the Convention in a "manner consistent with its federal role," recognizing that issues such as education are the responsibility of state and local governments; 2) the United States will not accept Convention obligations that restrict freedom of speech or expression; and 3) the United States and other States Parties may decide the nature of the health and family planning services referred to in the Convention, and may determine whether they are "necessary" and "appropriate" to distribute. The proposed Clinton Administration declarations included a "non-self-executing" provision, which proposed that no new laws would be created as a result of Convention ratification; and a "dispute settlement" provision, which stated that the United States was not bound by Convention Article 29(1), which refers unresolved disputes to the International Court of Justice.[16]

The Bush Administration has stated that it supports the Convention's goal of eradicating discrimination against women on a global scale, but has several concerns with the Convention itself.[17] These concerns were outlined in 2002, when the Senate Foreign Relations Committee held hearings on potential ratification of the Convention. Then-Secretary of State Colin Powell wrote a letter to the Foreign Relations Committee stating that the Convention was under State and Justice Departments review due to concerns regarding "the vagueness of the text of CEDAW and the record of the official U.N. body [the CEDAW Committee] that reviews and comments on the implementation."[18] In particular, the Administration cited "controversial interpretations" of the CEDAW Committee's recommendations to States Parties.[19] Powell's letter specifically noted a Committee report on Belarus that "questioned the celebration of mother's day,"[20] and a report on China that "called for legalized prostitution."[21] The Administration stated that these positions are "contrary to American law and sensibilities."[22]

The Administration argued that the vagueness of the text opened the door for broad interpretation by international and domestic entities, and contended that the 1994 RUDs did not address these interpretation issues. It also emphasized the importance of ensuring the Convention would not conflict with U.S. constitutional and statutory laws in areas typically controlled by the States.[23] In light of these concerns, the Administration urged the Foreign Relations Committee not to vote on the Convention until a full review was complete. The review began in mid-April 2002. On February 7, 2007, the Administration transmitted a letter to the Senate stating that it does not currently support the Senate taking action on the Convention.[24]

Senate Actions

The Convention has been pending in the Senate Foreign Relations Committee for over 25 years. The Committee held hearings in 1988 and 1990, but did not vote to recommend the Convention for advice and consent of the full Senate. With support from the Clinton Administration, the Senate held another round of ratification hearings in June 1994. The Committee reported the Convention favorably with a vote of 13 to 5 in September 1994, but the 103rd Congress adjourned before it could be brought to vote in the full Senate.[25] The Republicans were elected as the majority party in the 104th Congress, and the new Chairman of the Foreign Relations Committee, Senator Jesse Helms, did not allow further consideration of the CEDAW.

In June 2002, under the Chairmanship of Senator Joseph Biden, the Foreign Relations Committee once again held hearings on ratification of the Convention. The Committee heard testimony from non-governmental organizations, individuals from academia, public policy groups, and relevant agencies and organizations arguing for and against ratification.[26] On July 30, 2002, the Committee reported the Convention favorably by a vote of 12 to 7, subject to four reservations, five understandings, and two declarations.[27] These included the nine RUDs recommended by the Clinton Administration in 1994, plus two additional understandings. The additional understandings included a proposal from Senator Jesse Helms which stated that "nothing in this Convention shall be construed to reflect or create any right to abortion and in no case should abortion be promoted as a method of family planning." They also included a 2002 understanding sponsored by Senator Biden that stated, "the CEDAW Committee has no authority to compel parties to follow its recommendations." The 107th Congress adjourned before the Senate could vote on the Convention.

In subsequent years, the House of Representatives continued to demonstrate an interest in the Convention. On January 24, 2007, Representative Lynn Woolsey introduced a resolution expressing the sense of the House of Representatives that "the Senate should ratify the Convention on the Elimination of All Forms of Discrimination Against Women." The resolution currently has 93 cosponsors.[28] Representative Woolsey introduced similar legislation in the 109th, 108th, and 106th Congresses, with 115, 104, and 122 cosponsors, respectively.[29]

ISSUES FOR CONGRESS

This section addresses policy issues that emerged in the ongoing debate over U.S. ratification of the Convention. These issues may continue to play a role in the debate if the Senate considers the Convention during the 110th Congress.[30]

The Effectiveness of the Convention

A major point of contention among supporters and opponents of ratification is whether the Convention is an effective mechanism for addressing women's rights internationally. Proponents of the Convention, such as Representative Woolsey, describe the Convention as a "powerful tool" for women globally, and emphasize that the United States is the only industrialized country that has not ratified the Convention.[31] Advocates such as Senators Joseph Biden and Barbara Boxer argue that the Convention empowers women to achieve equality in their own countries, and cite specific examples of the Convention's success in achieving its purpose.[32] Some non-governmental organizations (NGOs) have also recorded the Convention's effectiveness in improving women's rights in specific countries and regions.[33]

Opponents of ratification recognize that global discrimination against women is a problem that should be eliminated, but they do not view the Convention as the most effective way to achieve this goal. Some contend that the Convention hurts rather than helps women struggling for human rights internationally. They argue that the Convention "serves as a facade for continuing atrocities," in countries that are State Parties to the Convention, such as China and North Korea.[34] Some opponents also contend that when considering treaty ratification, the Senate should act based on the standard of what is best for the American people.[35]

The Convention as an Instrument for U.S. Foreign Policy

Congressional and non-congressional supporters of the Convention contend that U.S. ratification will increase the credibility of the United States abroad and enhance its ability to champion women's rights in other countries.[36] The 2002 Foreign Relations Committee report stated that the United States should support ratification because, among other things, it "will give our diplomats a tool — a means to press other governments to fulfill their obligations under the Convention."[37] To illustrate this point, some ratification supporters cite a June 12, 2002 letter to the Foreign Relations Committee from Dr. Sima Samar, then-Afghan Minister of Women's Affairs. Dr. Samar asks the Senate to ratify the Convention, and says that "we will then be able to tell our countrymen that the United States, where women already have full legal rights, has just seen the need to ratify this treaty ... we will be able to refer to its terms and guidelines in public debates over what our laws should say."[38]

Opponents of this argument emphasize that the United States "has the strongest record on opportunities and rights for women in the world,"[39] and maintain the United States does not need to ratify the Convention to further its women's rights policies. In the minority views of the 2002 Foreign Relations Committee report, Senators Helms, Brownback, and Enzi stated that Afghan women were "relieved of the burden of an oppressive, anti-woman government" by "the personal heroism and sacrifice" of American forces, and not through a multilateral treaty such as CEDAW.

U.S. Sovereignty

The Senate has engaged in considerable debate over the impact of CEDAW ratification on U.S. sovereignty and international law. The minority views in the 2002 Senate Foreign Relations Committee report stated that the Convention represents "a disturbing international trend" of favoring international law over U.S. constitutional law and self-government, thereby undermining U.S. sovereignty. In particular, they were concerned that the Convention's description of discrimination against women is too broad, and that it may "apply to private organizations and areas of personal conduct not covered by U.S. law."[40]

Senators supporting the Convention maintain that ratification would not affect U.S. sovereignty. Senator Biden stated that the Convention will impose a "minimal burden" on the United States given that the U.S. Constitution and other existing federal and state laws already meet the obligations of the Convention. He also emphasized that the United States would file several RUDs to ensure that no new laws were created to meet the obligations of the Convention.[41]

Social Issues

Some opponents of ratification are concerned that the Convention may catalyze a pro-abortion movement in the United States and interfere with family rights such as marriage and parenting. They contend that the Convention is an effort to "redefine the family,"[42] and argue that CEDAW will "help lawyers and other pro-abortion advocates reach the goal of enshrining unrestricted access to abortion in the United States."[43] Some opponents are particularly concerned with the Convention's references to "family planning," and believe that U.S. ratification of the Convention will, among other things, undercut parental rights, and lead to gender re-education, homosexual rights, and legalized prostitution.[44]

Table 1. States Parties to the Convention on the Elimination of All Forms of Discrimination Against Women (as of November 2, 2006)

*ratified or acceded to the Optional Protocol		
Afghanistan	Gambia	Pakistan
Albania *	Georgia	Panama *
Algeria	Germany *	Papua New Guinea
Andorra *	Ghana	Paraguay *
Angola	Greece *	Peru *
Antigua and Barbuda *	Grenada	Philippines *
Argentina	Guatemala *	Poland *
Armenia *	Guinea	Portugal *
Australia	Guinea-Bissau	Republic of Korea *
Austria *	Guyana	Republic of Moldova *
Azerbaijan *	Haiti	Romania *
Bahamas	Honduras	Russian Federation *
Bahrain	Hungary *	Rwanda
Bangladesh *	Iceland *	Saint Kitts and Nevis
Barbados	India	Saint Lucia
Belarus *	Indonesia	St. Vincent and the Grenadines
Belgium *	Iraq	Samoa
Belize *	Ireland *	San Marino *
Benin	Israel	Sao Tome and Principe
Bhutan	Italy *	Saudi Arabia
Bolivia *	Jamaica	Senegal *
Bosnia and Herzegovina *	Japan	Serbia*
Botswana	Jordan	Seychelles
Brazil *	Kazakhstan *	Sierra Leone
Brunei Darussalam	Kenya	Singapore
Bulgaria *	Kiribati	Slovakia *
Burkina Faso *	Kuwait	Slovenia *
Burundi	Kyrgyzstan *	Solomon Islands *
Cambodia	Lao Peoples Democratic Rep.	South Africa *
Cameroon *	Latvia	Spain *
Canada *	Lebanon	Sri Lanka *
Cape Verde	Lesotho *	Suriname
Central African Republic	Liberia	Swaziland
Chad	Libyan A. Jamahiriya *	Sweden*
Chile	Liechtenstein *	Switzerland
China	Lithuania *	Syrian Arab Republic
Colombia *	Luxembourg *	Tajikistan

Table 1. (Continued)

*ratified or acceded to the Optional Protocol		
Cook Islands	Madagascar	Thailand *
Comoros	Malawi	The former Yugoslav Republic
Congo	Malaysia	Timor-Leste
Costa Rica *	Maldives *	Togo
Cote d'Ivoire	Mali *	Trinidad and Tobago
Croatia *	Malta	Tunisia
Cuba	Marshall Islands	Turkey *
Cyprus *	Mauritania	Turkmenistan
Czech Republic *	Mauritius	Tuvalu
Democratic People's Republic of Korea	Mexico *	Uganda
Democratic Republic of the Congo	Micronesia	Ukraine *
Denmark *	Monaco	United Arab Emirates
Djibouti	Mongolia *	United Kingdom *
Dominica	Montenegro *	United Republic of Tanzania *
Dominican Republic *	Morocco	Uruguay *
Ecuador *	Mozambique	Uzbekistan
Egypt	Myanmar	Vanuatu
El Salvador	Namibia *	Venezuela *
Equatorial Guinea	Nepal	Viet Nam
Eritrea	Netherlands *	Yemen
Estonia	New Zealand *	Zambia
Ethiopia	Nicaragua	Zimbabwe
Fiji	Niger *	
Finland *	Nigeria *	
France *	Norway *	
Gabon	Oman	

In response to criticism that ratification may impact family planning or abortion policy in the United States, some supporters emphasize that the word "abortion" is never mentioned in the Convention text. They refer to a 1994 State Department determination that the Convention is "abortion neutral," and contend that several of the RUDs proposed, such as the understandings on the CEDAW Committee and abortion, adequately address the concerns of ratification opponents concerned with family, abortion and family planning issues.[45]

Supporters of ratification also emphasize that countries where abortion is illegal, such as Ireland and Rwanda, have ratified the Convention.[46]

Administration Review of the Convention

Opponents of ratification object to Senate consideration of the Convention without a full legal and policy review from the Administration. In 2002 some Members of the Senate Foreign Relations Committee argued that the Senate should not consider the Convention without a new review from the State Department because "eight years of U.S. federal and state jurisprudence," had not yet been taken into account.[47] Senators representing the minority view recommended that the Senate "defer action on the Convention until the Administration's analysis and views are available."[48] A timetable for the review, which began in April 2002, was not put forward or agreed to at the hearing. On February 7, 2007, the State Department transmitted a letter to the Chairman of the Senate Committee on Foreign Relations identifying CEDAW as "a treaty on which the Administration does not support Senate Action at this time."[49]

REFERENCES

[1]   Women's rights and the equality of the sexes are addressed in general terms in the Universal Declaration of Human Rights, the International Covenant on Civil and Political Rights, and the International Covenant on Economic, Social, and Cultural Rights, among others.

[2]   See Table 1 for a full list of countries that are States Parties to the Convention and its Optional Protocol. The term "States Parties" refers to countries that have ratified or acceded to the Convention.

[3]   Article 28 of the Convention states that reservations can be filed as long as they are compatible with the "object and purpose" of the Convention. A full list of reservations by country can be found at [http://www.un.org/women watch/daw/ cedaw/ reservations.htm].

[4]   The Convention has been adopted by several U.S. state and local governments, including the California and Connecticut Senate, and the House of Representatives in Hawaii, South Dakota, and Illinois, among others. As of November 2005, the Convention has also been adopted by 18 counties and 44 cities.

[5] Drawn from "The Convention on the Elimination of All Forms of Discrimination Against Women," available at [http://www.un.org/women watch/daw/cedaw/text/ econvention.htm].

[6] Optional Protocols are often added to some treaties. The Optional Protocol for the Convention is a stand-alone treaty that can be signed and/or ratified by countries that are party to the main treaty. For more information on the Optional Protocol to the Convention, see [http://www.un.org/women watch/daw/cedaw/protocol/].

[7] More information on international treaty bodies relating to women's right is available at [http://www.un.org/womenwatch/asp/uscr/list.asp?ParcntID⁻ 1003].

[8] The Commission on the Status of Women was established in 1946 as a functional commission of the U.N. Economic and Social Council. It is responsible for preparing recommendations and reports for the Council on women's rights in the political, economic, and social realms. For more information, see [http://www.un.org/ womenwatch/daw/csw/].

[9] Some human rights treaties provide for a separate body to monitor implementation of the treaty by States Parties. The Committee was established under Article 17 of CEDAW, "for the purpose of considering the progress made in the implementation" of the Convention.

[10] Currently, the 23 experts come from Algeria, Bangladesh, Brazil, China, Croatia, Cuba, Egypt, France, Germany, Ghana, Israel, Italy, Jamaica, Japan, Malaysia, Mauritius, Netherlands, Portugal, Republic of Korea, Singapore, Slovenia, South Africa, and Thailand.

[11] As one of seven U.N. human rights treaty bodies, the CEDAW Committee is financed from the U.N. regular budget and is supported by the U.N. Division for the Advancement of Women.

[12] Under Article 21 of the Convention, the Committee shall, "make suggestions and general recommendations based on the examination of reports and information received from States Parties." A full list of CEDAW Committee recommendations can be found at [http://www. un.org/womenwatch/daw/cedaw/recommendations/index.html].

[13] The Committee considered an initial report from Tajikistan, and periodic reports from Austria, Azerbaijan, Colombia, Greece, India, Kazakhstan, Maldives, Namibia, Netherlands, Nicaragua, Peru, Poland, Suriname, and Vietnam.

[14] For further information on the 37th CEDAW Committee session, see [http://www.un.org/womenwatch/daw/cedaw/37sess.htm].

[15] RUDs refers to the "reservations, understandings, and declarations" that might accompany U.S. ratification of a treaty.

[16] For detailed descriptions of the RUDs, see U.S. Congress. Senate. Committee on Foreign Relations, "Convention on the Elimination of All Forms of Discrimination Against Women," Report, September 12, 1994. Washington, DC, Government Printing Office (Senate Exec. Rept. 103-38, 103d Congress, 2d Session), p. 6-8.

[17] "Statement by Ambassador Sichan Siv, U.S. Representative to the U.N. Economic and Social Council," U.S. Mission to the United Nations Press Release, October 30, 2003.

[18] Letter from Secretary of State Colin Powell to Senator Joseph Biden, Chairman of the Senate Foreign Relations Committee, July 8, 2002.

[19] Letter from Daniel J. Bryan, Assistant Attorney General, U.S. Department of Justice, to Senator Joseph Biden, Chairman of the Senate Foreign Relations Committee, July 26, 2002.

[20] U.N. document, A/55/38(SUPP), p. 37, paragraph 361 (2000).

[21] U.N. document, A/54/38/REV.1(SUPP), paragraphs 288-289, January 1, 1999.

[22] Letter from Daniel J. Bryan to Senator Joseph Biden, July 26, 2002.

[23] Ibid.

[24] Letter from Jeffrey T. Bergner, Assistant Secretary for Legislative Affairs, to Senator Joseph Biden, Chairman, Senate Committee on Foreign Relations, February 7, 2007.

[25] For more information on the 1994 hearings, see U.S. Congress. Senate. Committee on Foreign Relations, "Convention on the Elimination of All Forms of Discrimination Against Women," Report, September 12, 1994. Washington, DC, Government Printing Office (Senate Exec. Rept. 103-38, 103d Congress, 2d Session).

[26] Witnesses included Members of Congress, representatives from the World Family Policy Center, the American Enterprise Institute, Business and Professional Women/USA, and the former U.S. Representative to the U.N. Commission on the Status of Women.

[27] U.S. Congress. Senate. Committee on Foreign Relations, "Convention on the Elimination of All Forms of Discrimination Against Women," Report, September 6, 2002. Washington, DC, Government Printing Office (Senate Exec. Rept. 107-9, 107th Congress, 2d Session), p. 7-11.

[28] H.Res. 101 [110th], introduced January 24, 2007, by Representative Lynn Woolsey, referred to the Subcommittee on International Organizations,

Human Rights, and Oversight of the House Foreign Affairs Committee on February 5, 2007.

[29] H.Res. 67 [109th], introduced February 2, 2005; H.Res. 21 [108th], introduced January 7, 2003; and H.Res. 107 [106th], introduced March 10, 1999.

[30] Under the U.S. Constitution, the President is responsible for making treaties with the advice and consent of the Senate. Once the President transmits a treaty to the Senate, it is referred to the Committee on Foreign Relations. The House of Representatives plays a role in the treaty process only when separate legislation to implement the treaty is required. Thus, the issues for Congress discussed herein are issues that may be included in any consideration of the Convention by the Senate Foreign Relations Committee and/or the full Senate. See Article II, section 2 of the U.S. Constitution. More information on the treaty process is available at [http://www. senate.gov/artandhistory/history/common/briefing/Treaties.htm].

[31] *Congressional Record*, House of Representatives, June 16, 2005, H4612.

[32] Senators Joseph Biden and Barbara Boxer, "Op-Ed: Senate Needs to Ratify the Treaty for the Rights of Women," *San Francisco Chronicle*, June 13, 2002. Senators Biden and Boxer described a Tanzanian woman who reportedly "used the provisions of the treaty to ensure that she could sell land she inherited from her father, overcoming an initial court ruling which held that, as a woman, she could not sell land held by the clan."

[33] For example, Amnesty International examples of the Convention successes can be found at [http://www.amnestyusa.org/women/cedaw/world.html].

[34] Statement of Representative Juanita Millender-McDonald. U.S. Congress. Senate. Committee on Foreign Relations, "Treaty Doc. 96-53; Convention on the Elimination of All Forms of Discrimination Against Women." Hearing, June 13, 2002. 107th Congress, 2d Session. Washington, DC, U.S. Government Printing Office, 2002, S.Hrg. 107-530, p. 15.

[35] Additional Views of Senator Helms, Brownback, and Enzi. Statement of U.S. Congress. Senate. Committee on Foreign Relations, "Convention on the Elimination of All Forms of Discrimination Against Women," Report, September 6, 2002. Washington, DC, Government Printing Office (Senate Exec. Rept. 107-9, 107th Congress, 2d Session), p. 21.

[36] Human Rights Watch stated in a June 13, 2002 letter to the Senate Foreign Relations Committee, "By ratifying CEDAW, the U.S. government will be in a stronger position to support women's rights... Having not ratified CEDAW, U.S. intervention in support of women's rights may be construed

as 'cultural imperialism' or an 'American' agenda, as opposed to a rights-based approach."

[37] Committee Comments. U.S. Congress. Senate. Committee on Foreign Relations, "Convention on the Elimination of All Forms of Discrimination Against Women." Report, September 6, 2002. Washington, DC, Government Printing Office (Senate Exec. Rept. 107-9, 107th Congress, 2d Session), p. 5.

[38] Ibid, 6.

[39] Ibid, 16.

[40] Ibid, 16.

[41] U.S. Congress. Senate. Committee on Foreign Relations, "Treaty Doc. 96-53; Convention on the Elimination of All Forms of Discrimination Against Women." Hearing, June 13, 2003. 107th Congress, 2d Session. Washington, DC, U.S. Government Printing Office, 2002, S.Hrg. 107-530, p. 3.

[42] "Women for Faith and Family Statement on CEDAW," May 25, 2000, available at [http://www.wf-f.org/CEDAW.html].

[43] Additional Views of Senators Helms, Brownback, and Enzi. U.S. Congress. Senate. Committee on Foreign Relations, "Convention on the Elimination of All Forms of Discrimination Against Women" Report, September 6, 2002. Washington, DC, Government Printing Office, (Senate Exec. Rept. 107-9, 107th Congress, 2d Session), p. 22.

[44] The phrase "family planning" appears in the Introduction, Article 10(h), Article 12, and Article 14(b) of the Convention.

[45] "Myths and Realities: The U.N. Convention on the Elimination of All Forms of Discrimination Against Women," The United Nations Association of the United States of America, August 2002, available at [http://www.unausa.org/site/pp.asp?c= fvKRI8MPJpFand b=337341].

[46] "Letter to the Senate Foreign Relations Committee, Urging that CEDAW Move to the Full Senate," *Human Rights Watch,* July 29, 2002.

[47] "Letter to the Senate Foreign Relations Committee, Urging that CEDAW Move to the Full Senate," *Human Rights Watch,* July 29, 2002, p.20.

[48] Minority Views of Senators Helms, Lugar, Hagel, Frist, Allen, Brownback, and Enzi. U.S. Congress. Senate. Committee on Foreign Relations, "Convention on the Elimination of All Forms of Discrimination Against Women," Report, September 6, 2002. Washington, DC, Government Printing Office, (Senate Exec. Rept. 107-9, 107th Congress, 2d Session) p. 15.

[49] Letter from Jeffrey T. Bergner, Assistant Secretary for Legislative Affairs, to Senator Joseph Biden, Chairman, Senate Committee on Foreign Relations, February 7, 2007.

In: Sexual Discrimination and Harassment
Editor: Rachel C. Feldman, pp. 79-87
ISBN: 978-1-60456-380-1
© 2008 Nova Science Publishers, Inc.

Chapter 4

SEXUAL ORIENTATION DISCRIMINATION IN EMPLOYMENT: ANALYSIS OF H.R. 3685, THE EMPLOYMENT NON-DISCRIMINATION ACT OF 2007[*]

Edward Chan-Young Liu

ABSTRACT

H.R. 3685, passed by the House on November 7, 2007, would prohibit certain adverse employment actions taken against an individual because of that individual's actual or perceived sexual orientation. Referred to as the Employment NonDiscrimination Act of 2007 (ENDA), the bill also explicitly prohibits employment discrimination against an individual based upon the sexual orientation of persons associated with that individual, but does not permit disparate impact claims of sexual orientation discrimination. A substantial minority of states have enacted their own prohibitions against sexual orientation employment discrimination. Some instances of sexual orientation employment discrimination may also be prohibited by existing protections under Title VII of the Civil Rights Act of 1964, despite the fact that Title VII's definition of sex does not encompass sexual orientation. H.R. 3685 would also appear to exempt religious organizations as defined under Title VII.

---

[*] Excerpted from CRS Report RS22740, dated November 8, 2007.

OVERVIEW

On November 7, 2007, the House passed H.R. 3685, the Employment NonDiscrimination Act of 2007 (ENDA).[1] Apparently modeled after Title VII of the Civil Rights Act of 1964 (Title VII), ENDA, if enacted, would create the first federal prohibition against sexual orientation discrimination by private employers.[2] ENDA appears to represent one half of an earlier bill introduced by Representative Frank, which would have additionally prohibited employment discrimination on the basis of gender identity.[3] This report will discuss issues relating to employment discrimination on the basis of sexual orientation and specific provisions of ENDA.

EMPLOYMENT PRACTICES PROHIBITED BY ENDA

For the most part, the *types* of employment actions prohibited by ENDA dovetail with Title VII's prohibitions against discrimination on the basis of race, color, sex, national origin, and religion.[4] Notwithstanding this overall similarity, the text of ENDA does go beyond Title VII's text in two main ways: (1) prohibiting discrimination on *perceived* characteristics; and (2) textually creating associational rights under the act. That is not to say, however, that the protections of ENDA appear uniformly at least as extensive as Title VII's protections, as the bill explicitly *disallows* victims of sexual orientation discrimination from pursuing a disparate impact claim.[5] Each of these three differences is discussed in detail below.

Perceived Sexual Orientation Discrimination Is Prohibited

ENDA prohibits discrimination on the basis of actual or *perceived* sexual orientation.[6] The text of Title VII contains no comparable prohibition against discrimination on the basis of the *perceived* race, color, sex, national origin, or religion of a person. The Americans with Disabilities Act (ADA), however, does include in its definition of disability "*being regarded* as having a [physical or mental impairment]."[7] The semantic similarity between "perceived" and "regarded" suggests that existing judicial interpretation of that language in the ADA may be instructive for courts, agencies or employers attempting to interpret what is meant by "perceived sexual orientation." In other words, to the extent that "being regarded" as disabled under the ADA has been held to require an examination of an *employer's* subjectively held beliefs, courts may interpret ENDA to require the same.[8]

Associational Rights Are Protected

H.R. 3685 prohibits adverse employment actions taken against an individual on the basis of the actual or perceived sexual orientation of a person who associates with that individual.[9] Although Title VII contains no analogous text, associational rights under Title VII have been recognized by federal courts in the context of interracial marriage.[10]

Disparate Sexual Orientation Impact Claims Are Disallowed

Section 4(g) of ENDA disallows disparate impact claims on the basis of sexual orientation. Therefore, whereas a Title VII claim could proceed where the plaintiff showed that a particular job requirement disproportionately impacted one racial or religious group, ENDA does not appear to allow a plaintiff to show that a particular job requirement disproportionately impacts one sexual orientation over another.[11]

SEX VS. SEXUAL ORIENTATION

ENDA defines sexual orientation as "homosexuality, heterosexuality, or bisexuality."[12] In contrast, Title VII's prohibition against discrimination on the basis of sex has consistently been interpreted to exclude discrimination on the basis of sexual orientation.[13] However, courts have held that the fact that a victim of discrimination is homosexual or bisexual does not preclude a claim under Title VII. In some cases, victims of treatment that would arguably *also* qualify as sexual orientation discrimination, may be able to successfully assert that they were victims of sexual harassment or sex stereotyping under Title VII.

Sexual Harassment

In the context of sexual harassment, recent court decisions have been guided by the Supreme Court's decision in *Oncale v. Sundowner Offshore Services*.[14] In that case, a male employee suffered physical abuse of a sexual nature, but his claims of sexual harassment were initially denied by Fifth Circuit precedent which held that same-sex sexual harassment is not actionable under Title VII. The Supreme Court reversed, holding that, in cases of alleged sexual harassment, the gender of the victim and harasser are not dispositive, but rather the critical question is whether the harassment occurred "because of sex."[15] The Court also recognized that an inference that harassment is "because of sex" is not obvious where the harasser and the victim are of the same sex,[16]but provided three examples of how such an inference could be established: (1) if the harasser sexually desired the victim; (2) if the harasser was hostile to the presence of one sex in the workplace; or (3) if comparative data showed that the harasser targeted only members of one sex.[17]

The Ninth Circuit appears to have further held, in *Rene v. MGM Grand Hotel*, that harassment "which targeted body parts clearly linked to [a person's] sexuality" constituted sexual discrimination prohibited by Title VII.[18] Even though the victim believed he was harassed because of his *sexual orientation*, the court held that "whatever else those attacks may, or may not, have been 'because of' has no legal consequence."[19] Although the plaintiff in *Rene* prevailed, the holding of the Ninth Circuit may contradict the Supreme Court's earlier holding in *Oncale*. As the dissent in *Rene* noted, the Ninth Circuit relied in large part on *Doe v. City of Belleville*, in which the Seventh Circuit argued that evidence of physical abuse of a sexual nature alone could lead to an inference that the victim was targeted because of his gender.[20] That judgment, however, was vacated and remanded to the Seventh Circuit after the Court's decision in *Oncale*.[21] The text of the opinion in *Oncale* also seems to require more than conduct of a sexual nature in order to give rise to an inference that it was "because of sex."[22]

Sex Stereotypes

Based upon the Supreme Court's opinion in *Price Waterhouse v. Hopkins*, victims of sexual orientation discrimination may also prevail under Title VII, where the facts *also* indicate the presence of discrimination for failure to conform to sex stereotypes.[23] In *Price Waterhouse*, a female employee was denied partnership in an accounting firm, despite the fact that she was regarded as a high performer.[24] Furthermore, partners in the firm had instructed her to act more femininely in order to be considered for a partnership in the future.[25] The Court held that Price Waterhouse was applying standards for partnership in a prohibited sexually disparate manner, in that Title VII did not permit an employer to evaluate female employees based upon their conformity with the employer's stereotypical view of femininity.[26]

Relying on *Price Waterhouse*, the Third Circuit held, in *Bibby v. Phila. Coca Cola Bottling Co.*, that harassment of an individual for failure to conform to sex stereotypes could constitute harassment "because of sex" consistent with *Oncale*.[27] Furthermore, the court held that harassment for failure to conform to gender stereotypes is still "because of sex" even if the animosity towards nonconformance is caused by a belief that such behavior indicates homosexuality.[28]

Therefore, based upon the decisions in *Rene v. MGM Grand Hotel* and *Bibby v. Coca Cola*, one could conclude that certain types of sexual orientation discrimination are currently prohibited under Title VII.[29] However, one should *not* take this to mean that ENDA does not purport to prohibit conduct not already prohibited by Title VII. For example, were an employer simply to require job applicants to state his or her sexual orientation on a job application, and consequently refused to hire applicants that indicated they were homosexuals, it is not clear that this would be prohibited by Title VII's existing provisions. However, such actions would almost certainly be prohibited by a plain reading of ENDA.

RELIGIOUS ORGANIZATIONS UNDER ENDA

ENDA states that its provisions do not apply to "religious organizations" as defined under Title VII.[30] Similarly, religious organizations would likely remain free from claims of any discrimination with respect to their selection of clergy and certain other positions related to worship.

The "Ministerial Exception"

At a minimum, ENDA would likely not apply to religious organizations' selection of clergy or other positions involved in worship or ritual. Discrimination on the basis of race, sex, national origin or religion has been held to be permissible, in these positions, under the judicially created "ministerial exception" to Title VII. This exception was created to reconcile some of Title VII's prohibitions with the Free Exercise Clause of the Federal Constitution. It has been adopted in eight Federal Circuits and applies to employees whose "primary duties include teaching, spreading the faith, church governance, supervision of a religious order, or supervision of participation in religious ritual and worship."[31] This exception to Title VII allows discrimination on the basis of any characteristic, including race and sex, but only with respect to "a religious institution's choice as to who will perform spiritual functions."[32] Because the rationale for this exception is derived from the Federal Constitution, and not the text of Title VII, it would likely be wholly applicable to ENDA as well.

Statutory Exemptions

In addition, ENDA states that its prohibitions will not apply to religious organizations as they are defined under Title VII.[33] Title VII exempts religious organizations generally, as well as educational institutions that are either substantially owned by a religious organization or directed towards the propagation of a particular religion.[34] Federal courts have interpreted Title VII to require an inquiry into whether an entity's "purpose and character are primarily religious" in order to qualify as a religious entity.[35] Most recently, in September of 2007, the Third Circuit identified nine factors other courts have considered when determining if an institution is religious, none of which are determinative.[36] This statutory exemption appears to apply to a much broader group of entities than the ministerial exception, which only applies to specific positions with a close nexus to ritual or worship activities.

REFERENCES

[1]   Employment Non-Discrimination Act of 2007, H.R. 3685, 110th Cong. (2007).

[2]   A substantial minority of states have enacted laws prohibiting sexual orientation discrimination. *See, e.g.,* GAO Report, *infra* note 12. Additionally, Executive Order 13,087 prohibits sexual orientation discrimination against federal executive branch employees. Exec. Order No. 13,087, 3 C.F.R. 191 (1998).

[3]   Employment Non-Discrimination Act of 2007, H.R. 2015, 110th Cong. (2007). Gender identity is defined by H.R. 2015 as "the gender-related

identity, appearance, or mannerisms or other gender-related characteristics of an individual, with or without regard to the individual's designated sex at birth." For a discussion of issues related to gender identity discrimination, see CRS Report RL34242, *Gender Identity Discrimination in Employment: Analysis of H.R. 3686 in the 110th Congress*, by Edward Chan-Young Liu.

[4]   *Compare* H.R. 3685 § 4(a-d) *with* Civil Rights Act of 1964, P.L. 88-352, tit. vii, § 703(a-d) (codified at 42 U.S.C. § 2000e-2(a-d)). H.R. 3685 also limits applicability to those employers with 15 or more employees, as does the current version of Title VII. *Compare* H.R. 3685 § 3(a)(4)(A) *with* 42 U.S.C. § 2000e(b).

[5]   H.R. 3685 § 4(g).

[6]   H.R. 3685 § 4(a-f).

[7]   42 U.S.C. § 12102(2)(C).

[8]   For further discussion of the definition of disability under the ADA, *see*, CRS Report RL33304, *The Americans with Disabilities Act (ADA): The Definition of Disability*, by Nancy Lee Jones.

[9]   H.R. 3685 § 4(e).

[10] E.g., Parr v. Woodmen of the World Life Ins. Co., 791 F.2d 888, 891-892 (11th Cir. 1986).

[11] For an example of how a disparate impact claim of racial discrimination is established under Title VII, see *Griggs v. Duke Power Co.*, 401 U.S. 424 (1971).

[12] The bill does not define these terms, although the terms are defined elsewhere in the U.S. Code, in the context of the military. 10 U.S.C. § 654(f) (2007). Among the states that do prohibit discrimination on the basis of sexual orientation, it is almost universally defined as including homosexuality, bisexuality, or heterosexuality. *See,* GOV'T ACCOUNTING OFFICE, *Sexual Orientation-Based Employment Discrimination: States' Experience with Statutory Prohibitions* at 2-4, tbl.1, July 9, 2002, available at [http://www.gao.gov/new.items/d02878r.pdf].

[13] See, Ulane v. Eastern Airlines, 742 F.2d 1081 (8th Cir. 1984); DeSantis v. Pacific Telephone and Telegraph Co., 608 F.2d 237 (9th Cir. 1979); Holloway v. Arthur Andersen, 566 F.2d 659 (9th Cir. 1977).

[14] Oncale v. Sundowner Offshore Services, 523 U.S. 75 (1998).

[15] *Id.* at 77, 81.

[16] The Court did note, however, that in the related context of racial discrimination it has never *presumed* that members of one race will not discriminate against other members of the same race. *Id.* at 78.

[17] *Id.* at 80-81. This discussion of *Oncale* is not meant to imply that sexual orientation·harassment is only perpetrated by persons of the same sex as the victim, but merely to suggest that an employer's assertion that harassment occurred solely because of sexual orientation, and not sex, may be refuted by the methods of proof offered in *Oncale.*

[18] *Rene v. MGM Grand Hotel*, 305 F.3d 1061, 1066 (9th Cir. 2002). In this case, the court found that the sexual nature of the harassers' attacks, which were directed at the victim's crotch and anus, readily gave rise to the inference that he was targeted because of his sex. *Id.* at 1065.

[19] *Id.* at 1064, 1066.

[20] *Id.* at 1066 (citing *Doe v. City of Belleville*, 119 F.3d 563, 580 (7th Cir. 1997)).

[21] City of Belleville v. Doe, 523 U.S. 1001 (1998).

[22] "[The plaintiff] must always prove that the conduct at issue was not merely tinged with offensive sexual connotations." *Oncale*, 523 U.S. at 81.

[23] Price Waterhouse v. Hopkins, 490 U.S. 228 (1989).

[24] *Id.* at 233-234

[25] *Id.* at 235.

[26] *Id.* at 250-251.

[27] Bibby v. Phila. Coca Cola Bottling Co., 260 F.3d 257, 264 (3rd Cir. 2001).

[28] *Id.* at 265.

[29] Note that § 15 of H.R. 3685 states that the act will not be construed to invalidate or limit the rights under any other Federal or state law. Therefore, to the extent that sexual orientation discrimination is prohibited under Title VII or state law, it may remain so if ENDA is enacted.

[30] H.R. 3685 §§ 3(a)(8) and 6. See also, CRS Report RS22745, Religion and the Workplace: Legal Analysis of Title VII of the Civil Rights Act of 1964 as It Applies to Religious Organizations, by Cynthia Marie Brougher.

[31] *Petruska v. Gannon Univ.*, 462 F.3d 294, 304 (3rd Cir. 2006) (citing favorable opinions in the 4th, 5th, 7th, 8th, 9th, 11th, and D.C. Circuits).

[32] *Petruska v. Gannon*, 462 F.3d at 305.

[33] H.R. 3685 §§ 3(a)(8), 6 (explicitly adopting the definition of religious organizations in Title VII).

[34] 42 U.S.C. §§ 2000e-1(a), 2000e-2(e)(2).

[35] *EEOC v. Townley Eng'g and Mfg. Co.*, 859 F.2d 610, 618 (9th Cir. 1988). *See also EEOC v. Kamehameha Schools*, 990 F.2d 458, 461 (9th Cir. 1993).

[36] *LeBoon v. Lancaster Jewish Comm. Ctr. Ass'n.*, 2007 U.S. App. LEXIS 22328, 19-20 (3rd Cir. 2007) "(1) whether the entity operates for a profit, (2) whether it produces a secular product, (3) whether the entity's articles of

incorporation or other pertinent documents state a religious purpose, (4) whether it is owned, affiliated with or financially supported by a formally religious entity such as a church or synagogue, (5) whether a formally religious entity participates in the management, for instance by having representatives on the board of trustees, (6) whether the entity holds itself out to the public as secular or sectarian, (7) whether the entity regularly includes prayer or other forms of worship in its activities, (8) whether it includes religious instruction in its curriculum, to the extent it is an educational institution, and (9) whether its membership is made up by coreligionists." *Id*

INDEX

U

V

W

Y

Z

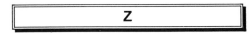